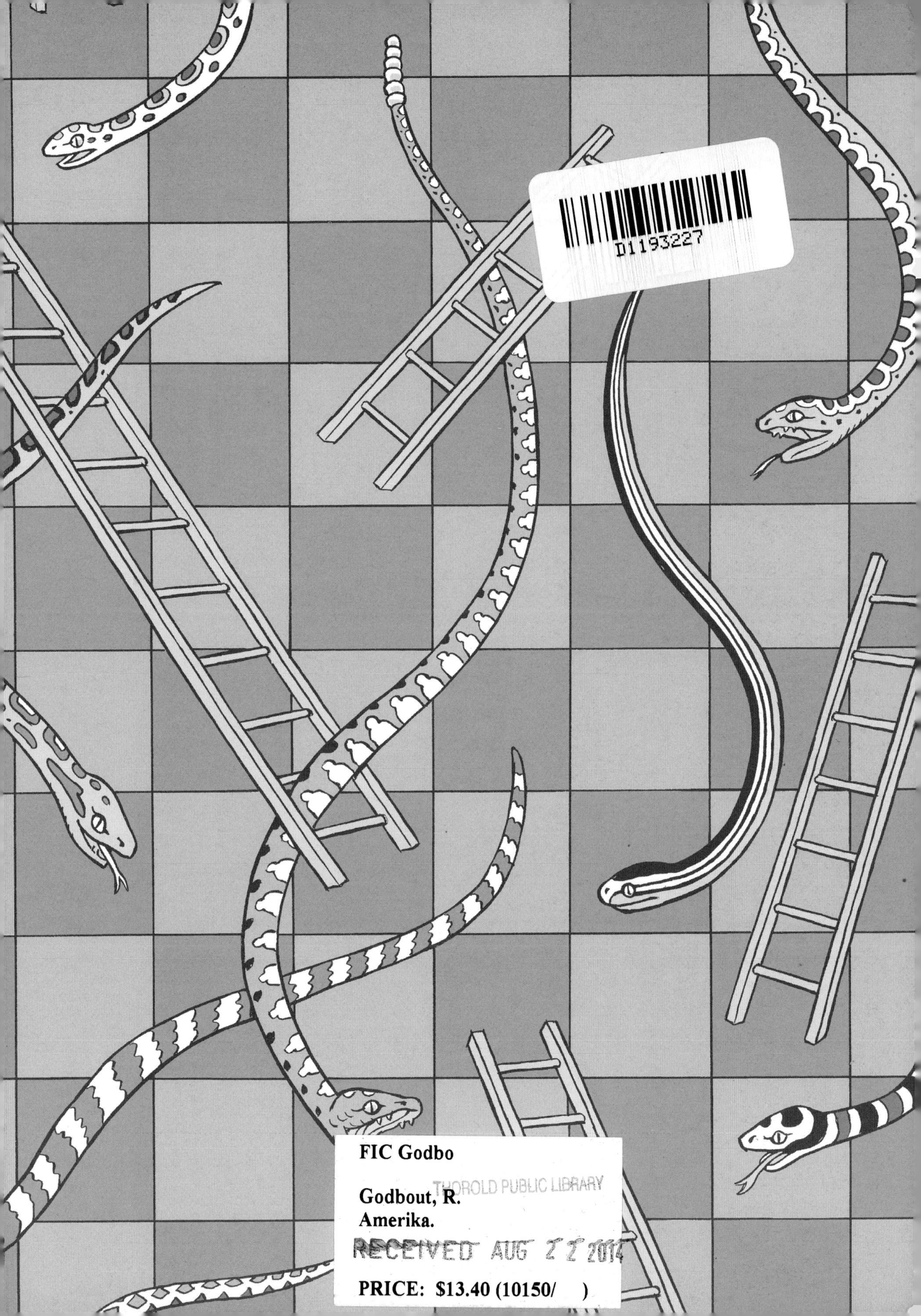

AMERIKA

First English Edition
Original French edition © Réal Godbout, Les Éditions de la Pastèque

Translation by Helge Dascher
Editorial assistance by Rupert Bottenberg
Font production by Tracy Hurren

BDANG logo by Billy Mavreas
BDANG Imprint edited by Andy Brown

Printed by Gauvin Press in Quebec, Canada

Library and Archives Canada Cataloguing in Publication

Godbout, Réal
[L'Amérique, ou Le disparu. English]
      Amerika / Réal Godbout ; translated by Helge Dascher.

Based on the novel by Franz Kafka.
Translation of L'Amérique, ou Le disparu, published by
Les Editions de la Pastèque, 2013.
ISBN 978-1-894994-81-1 (pbk.)

      1. Kafka, Franz, 1883-1924--Adaptations. 2. Graphic novels.
I. Dascher, Helge, 1965-, translator II. Title. III. Title: L'Amérique,
ou Le disparu. English

PN6734.A4413G63 2014   741.5'971   C2014-900406-0

BDANG IMPRINT #13

Conundrum Press
Greenwich, Nova Scotia, Canada
www.conundrumpress.com

Conundrum Press acknowledges the financial support of the Canada Council for the Arts and the
Government of Canada, through the Canada Book Fund, toward its publishing activities. We acknowledge
the financial support of the Government of Canada, through the National Translation Program for Book
Publishing, for our translation activities.

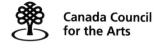

AMERIKA

BASED ON THE NOVEL BY FRANZ KAFKA

RÉAL GODBOUT

BDANG

Chapter 1
THE STOKER

Als der siebzehnjährige Karl Roßmann, der von seinen arme[n]
[n]ach Amerika geschickt worden war, weil ihn ein Dienstmäd[chen]
[u]nd ein Kind von ihm bekommen hatte, in dem schon langsa[m]
[S]chiff in d[en Hafen vo]n Newyork einfuhr, erblickte er die sch[on]
[b]eobachtete Statue der [Freiheitsg]öttin wie in einem plötzlich
[ge]wordenen S[onnenlicht]. Ihr Arm mit dem Schwert ragte wie
[e]mpor und um ihre Gestalt wehten die freien Lüfte. "So hoch",
[sag]d wurde, wie er so gar nicht an das Weggehn dachte, von de[r]
[an]schwellenden Menge der Gepäckträger, die an ihm vorüber[...]
[all]mählich bis an das Bordgeländer geschoben. Ein junger Ma[nn]
[w]ährend der Fahrt flüchtig bekannt geworden war sagte im V[...]
[j]a haben Sie denn noch keine Lust auszusteigen?" "Ich bin do[ch]
[sa]gte Karl ihn anlachend und hob, aus Übermut und weil er ei[n]
[ju]nge war, den Koffer auf die Achsel. Aber wie er über seinen [...]
[a]nsah, der ein wenig seinen Stock schwenkend sich schon mit [...]
[ent]fernte, merkte er, daß er seinen Regenschirm unten im Sch[iff]
[...]te. Er bat schnell den Bekannten, der nicht sehr beglückt sc[hien]
[fr]eundlichkeit, bei seinem Koffer einen Augenblick zu warten,
[sch]nell die Situation um sich bei der Rückkehr zurechtzufinde[n]
[v]on. Unten fand er zu seinem Bedauern einen Gang, der seine[n]
[ab]kürzt hätte, zum erstenmal versperrt, was wahrscheinlich [mit der Aus]
[...]schiffung sämtlicher Passagiere zusammenhieng, und muß[te]
[sei]nen Weg durch eine Unzahl kleiner Räume, fortwährend abbi[egende]
[Kor]ridore, kurze Treppen, die einander aber immer wieder folgt[en]
[ein]es Zimmer mit einem verlassenen Schreibtisch mühselig suc[hen]
[...] tatsächlich, da er diesen Weg nur ein oder zweimal und imm[er in]
[grö]ßerer Gesellschaft gegangen war, ganz und gar verirrt hatte.
[...]osigkeit und da er keinen Menschen traf und nur immerfort
[das] Scharren der tausend Menschenfüße hörte und von der Fern[e]
[...]ch das letzte Arbeiten der schon eingestellten Maschine me[...]
[...] zu überlegen, an eine beliebige kleine Türe zu [...]

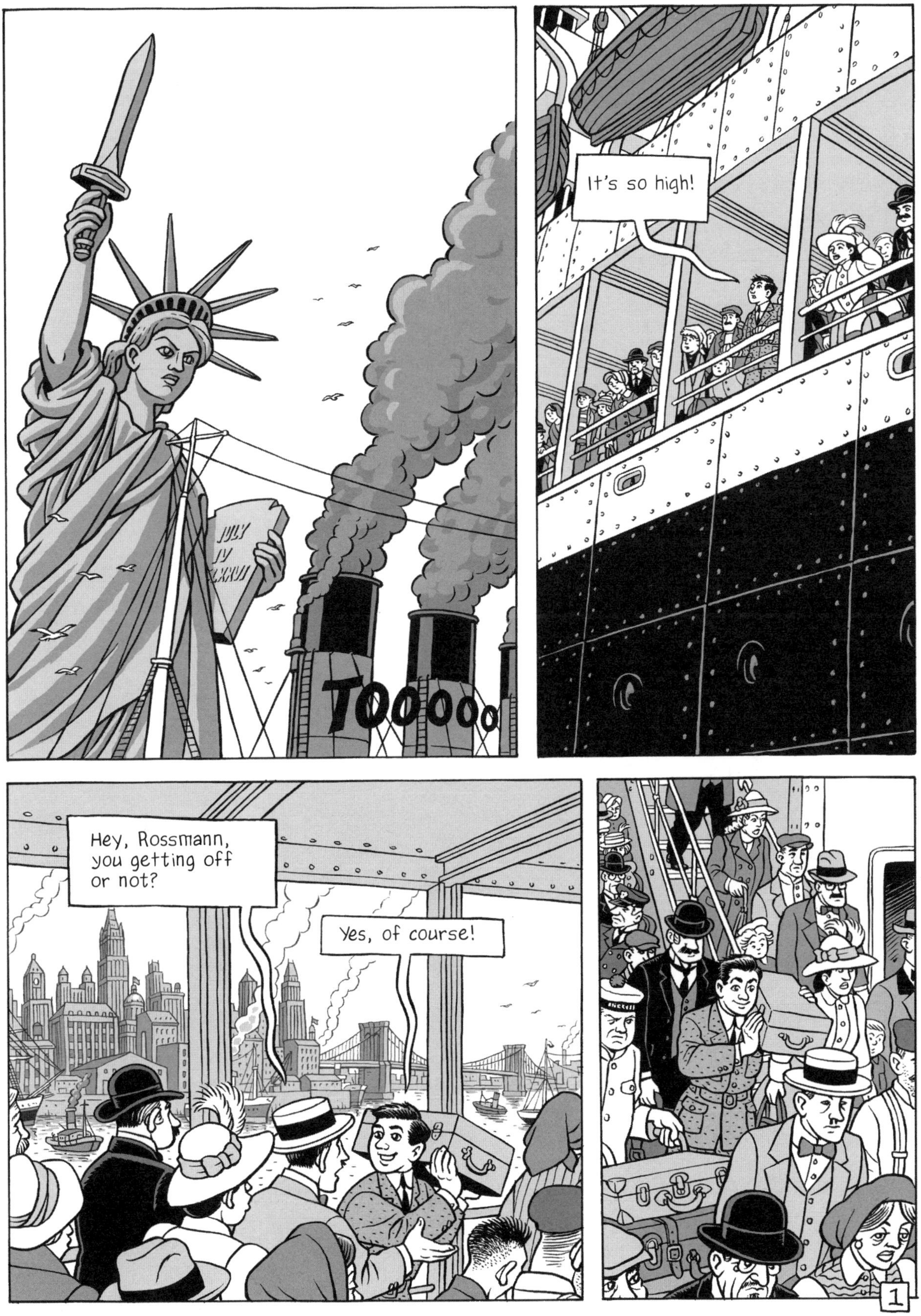
TOOOOo
It's so high!
Hey, Rossmann, you getting off or not?
Yes, of course!
1

MY UMBRELLA!

I forgot my umbrella! I need to go back down to get it. Would you mind keeping an eye on my trunk for a moment? I'll be right back.

But...

Excuse me...

Sorry...

Can't pass here, sir.

Maybe this way...

I never realized during the voyage what a big ship this is!

I'm totally lost. I'll need to ask for help.

Maybe here...

IT'S OPEN!

KNOCK KNOCK

I'm not bothering you?

Don't just stand there. Come in and shut the door. I hate it when people can see into the cabin!

But everybody's left...

That's not the point.

I came downstairs to get my umbrella and I've lost my way. I left my trunk with an acquaintance. His name is... uh... Butterbaum. Yes, that's it, Butterbaum... I need to hurry, he must be wondering where I am!

Your trunk is probably gone by now. And your umbrella too. This is New York, you know... Just stay here a bit. If your things are still onboard, they'll be easier to find once the ship is empty.

Talk about bad luck... And to think I've watched over that trunk day and night since we left Hamburg...

Karl, my dear boy, take care of that trunk. It's all you have now.

I wonder how long it'll take him to lose it.

...are you on your own?

Yes, I'm on my own.

... all alone, and this man I hardly know may be the only friend that I have...

Uh...do you know this ship well?

You bet! I'm the stoker.

You are? I've always been interested in machines! I was studying to be an engineer back home in Europe, before I was forced to go to America.... I'd love to be a stoker.

WANT MY JOB, IS THAT IT? GO AHEAD, TAKE IT! I've had it with this damn ship and the lousy treatment I get here!

What do you mean?

This is a German ship, right? So tell me how come the chief mechanic, Schubal, a *Romanian*, a real scoundrel, is on my back all the time? Or why he's always harassing and insulting me? I've served on every sea in the world—I know this trade better than anybody. Does that make sense to you?

No, that's not fair at all. You should talk to the captain about it..

The captain! **HA!** Think the captain's gonna listen to me? Grow up, boy! Get out—go run after your trunk instead of sitting around giving bad advice!

I'm sorry.

4

Hear that? Not a sound. The passengers have all left. We can go up now.

Where are we going?

To see the captain.

??

Wanna meet me later, gorgeous?

Hey, where'd you find that pretty boy?

Hee-hee!

Here goes.

Come in.

KNOCK
KNOCK
KNOCK

Yes? How can I help you?

I... I would like to speak with the cap... the purser, please.

These gentlemen wish to speak with the purser, Sir.

The purser is not available right now.

5

Get out. You've got no business here.

You can't just turn us away!

We're here to present the case of this gentleman, the stoker, who is the victim of constant harassment by his superior, the chief mechanic Schubal!

What?

It's true, he's always out to get me.

I know that man, Captain. A real trouble-maker. All he ever does is complain.

Let's hear him out anyway.

But the stoker's listeners soon lose interest in his grievances.

He's really not helping his case! I'll have to step in...

Mr. Schubal is unfair incompet work overtime intolerable insulting and back hurt enough this ution of task is work shift sent me to cle the toilets even th it wasn't m their man Schubal the Romanians a host dishonest favouritism an day threatened m had enough

Listen, you need to sort out your complaints and explain them more clearly. These gentlemen are very busy— we shouldn't be testing their patience.

!

WHO ASKED YOU? I CAN HANDLE THIS ALL BY MYSELF!

That's enough! We've wasted too much time already!

ONE MOMENT!

6

What's your name, young man?

Me? Well, uh, my na...

KNOCK KNOCK KNOCK

Come in!

Mr. Schubal! We were just talking about you.

Huh?

Yes, captain, I heard there was trouble. I'm ready to defend myself against all accusations brought against me by this individual. I have papers here to support my claims, and I've brought a few impartial witnesses who can corroborate my statements, if necessary. They're right outside the door.

Liar!

We'll settle this matter later. For now, I believe Mr. Jacob wanted an answer to his question...

Go ahead, tell us your name?

Karl Rossmann.

KARL ROSSMANN?!?

But then...

YOU'RE MY NEPHEW!!

Well, I do have an uncle in America, according to my parents. But Jacob is his first name. His family name would be the same as my mother's maiden name, which is...

BENDELMAYER! See? I really am your uncle! I cut all ties to my family long ago, and when I became an American citizen, I changed my name to Edward Jacob.

SENATOR Edward Jacob.

Young man, I wonder if you know how lucky you are. You've got a brilliant future ahead of you!

But...how come...?

I think an explanation is called for. Gentlemen, to put it simply, my nephew's parents turned him out the way you'd get rid of a bothersome cat, for an incident that can hardly be considered his fault...

Ahem

He was seduced—yes, *seduced* is the right word in this case—by a house-maid who had a child by him. Karl's parents...

Oh!

Ah!

...wishing to avoid a scandal and possible financial claims, decided to pack him off to America with nothing but his meager baggage to call his own.

How could he possibly know?

snif

What did he say?

Karl would be just one more poor immigrant today, with nothing to fall back on—I'm not even sure Immigration would have let him enter the country—if the maid, a certain Johanna Brummer, had not decided to write to me, out of affection for Karl, to tell me he was on his way.

The sight of the letter brings back memories Karl would have preferred to forget....

Come...

Karl... OH, KARL!

It all happened so fast....

...and that's how you find a long-lost nephew! Great story, isn't it?

9

And now, Karl, I want to hear you say, right here in front of everybody, that I'm your uncle.

You are my uncle...

Come here, my dear nephew! You've got nothing to worry about anymore! I'll see to your education, my boy!

BRAVO
CLAP CLAP CLAP

Congratulations, young man!

I'm delighted for you!

CLAP CLAP CLAP CLAP

Hear hear!

I'm happy, too, but...what about the stoker? What will happen to him?

That's up to the captain to decide.

Why don't you speak up? How come you let them push you around?

Well...

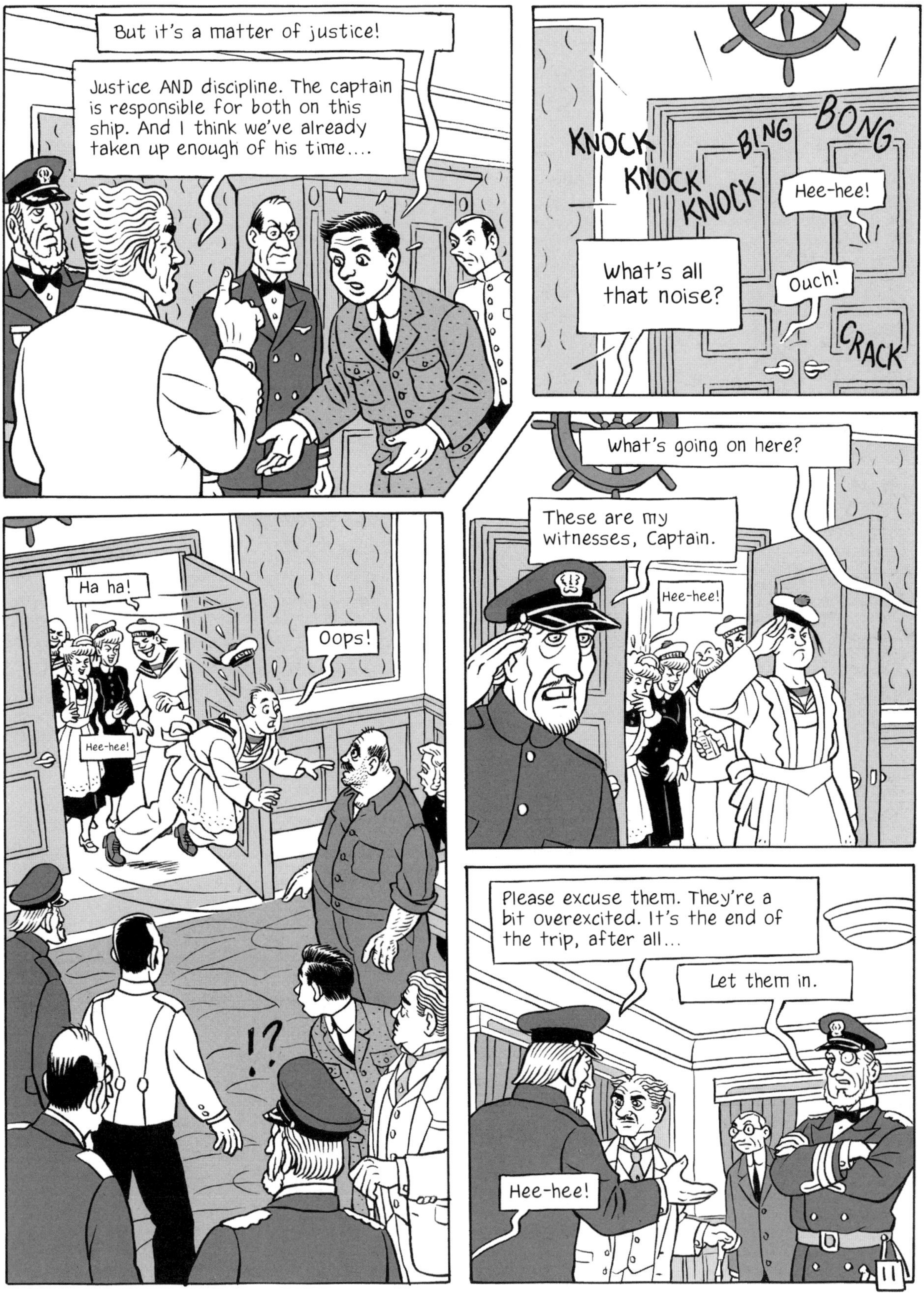
But it's a matter of justice!
Justice AND discipline. The captain is responsible for both on this ship. And I think we've already taken up enough of his time....
KNOCK
KNOCK
KNOCK
BING
BONG
Hee-hee!
What's all that noise?
Ouch!
CRACK
What's going on here?
These are my witnesses, Captain.
Hee-hee!
Ha ha!
Oops!
Hee-hee!
!?
Please excuse them. They're a bit overexcited. It's the end of the trip, after all...
Let them in.
Hee-hee!
11

Well, Sir, it's time for us to bid you farewell. It was a pleasure, Captain.

Hee...

Likewise, Senator. I hope we have the opportunity to see each other again soon under equally auspicious circumstances.

Indeed. But I think one nephew is quite enough for now...heh heh!

Please show the Senator and his nephew the way.

You've got a new life ahead of you, Karl.

m Hause des Onkels gewöhnte sich Karl bald an die neuen
Verhältnisse. Der Onkel kam ihm aber auch in jeder Kleinigkei
reundlich entgegen und niemals mußte Karl sich erst durch so
rfahrungen belehren lassen, wie dies meist das erste Leben in
usland so verbittert. Karls Zimmer lag im sechsten Stockwer
auses, dessen fünf untere Stockwerke, an welche sich in der T
ei unterirdische anschlossen, von dem Geschäftsbetrieb des O
ngenommen wurden. Das Licht, das in sein Zimmer durch zw
nster und eine Balkontüre eindrang, brachte Karl immer wie
aunen, wenn er des Morgens aus seiner kleinen Schlafkamme
ntrat. Wo hätte er wohl wohnen müssen, wenn er als armer kle
nwanderer ans Land gestiegen wäre? Ja vielleicht hätte man
s der Onkel nach seiner Kenntnis der Einwanderungsgesetze
sehr wahrscheinlich hielt, gar nicht in die Vereinigten Staat
gelassen sondern ihn nach Hause geschickt, ohne sich weiter
um zu kümmern, daß er keine Heimat mehr hatte. Denn auf
fte man hier nicht hoffen und es war ganz richtig, was Karl in
sicht über Amerika gelesen hatte; nur die Glücklichen schiene
Glück zwischen den unbekümmerten Gesichtern ihrer Umgeb
rhaft zu genießen. Ein schmaler Balkon zog sich vor dem Zim
er ganzen Länge nach hin. Was aber in der Heimatstadt Karls
höchste Aussichtspunkt gewesen wäre, gestattete hier nicht v
r als den Überblick über eine Straße, die zwischen zwei Reihe
lich abgehackter Häuser gerade und darum wie fliehend in d
e sich verlief, wo aus vielem Dunst die Formen einer Kathedr
eheuer sich erhoben.

Chapter 2:
THE UNCLE

Days have passed.

As he does most mornings...

...Karl looks out and marvels...

COB & co

13

...at the spectacle of the street.

You want to be careful, Karl.

The bustle of a big city is often a fascinating thing for those who are only visiting. But that fascination can become dangerous for someone who wants to stay.

If you give in to it, you risk losing yourself!

Everything is new for you here, and there's so much to see and discover. You can't assimilate it all at once.

You see, Karl, a new immigrant is like a newborn. But there's no need for you to worry—it will take you much less time to get used to the American way of life than it takes a baby to adapt to the world of humans.

There's more to see than what's outside that window. Quick, get dressed. I've got something for you.

You do?

Here's your new desk, Karl. It's the very latest model. I hope it'll help you in your studies.

Oh, uncle! Thank you!

It's magnificent! ... All these compartments! I bet even the president doesn't have one like this!

They don't make them any better! And that's not all. Look...

15

You just turn the handle...

CRRRRRR

...and the compartments rearrange themselves.

BZZZZZT

CLAC

CLIC

CRRRRRR

Amazing!

It reminds me of the nativity scenes in Prague, when I was a child...

But don't overdo it! The parts are fragile and very expensive to repair. In fact, I'd advise you not to use it all.

Ah...

Despite his measured and frugal ways, the senator spares no expense in pleasing his nephew.

Tell me, Karl, what were your favourite pastimes back in Europe?

Well, uh...

I played a bit of piano... Or at least I tried to. My mother taught me how.

To keep from spoiling Karl, his uncle holds off on granting what would appear to be a request. But after a week...

For ME?! Oh, uncle, it's MAGNIFICENT!

Not at all.

16

So, Karl, want to play us a little something?

Let's see... I remember this one old tune from back home... It's a military march.

PLINK PLINK PLONK PLINK

PLONK PLINK PLONK PLINK

PLINK PLOINK OUPS! PLONK PLINK PLONK

Hmm! ...Well, if you'd like to give the violin or the French horn a try too, just say so.

Thank you! That's very kind of you!

In the meantime, you should get to work on these...

The Star Spangled Banner
WORDS & MUSIC BY FRANCIS SCOTT KEY

JOHN PHILIP SOUSA'S Great Marches
PIANO TRANSCRIPTIONS BY JO...

But of course most of Karl's time is dedicated to learning English.

...my uncle is rich...

You've made excellent progress, Karl! It's time you got to know some people. Your English teacher will be at your side, just in case.

17

Which is how Karl comes to meet Mr. Mack, the leisured and athletic son of a millionaire.

I am very happy to meet you.

Do you ride? I go out every morning. You should come along.

But I've never been on a horse.

That's not a problem! I'll teach you.

I'll have to ask my uncle first.

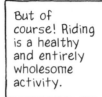

But of course! Riding is a healthy and entirely wholesome activity.

And so, every morning at dawn, just before his English lesson...

Uncle, I have two favours to ask you.

Go ahead.

First, could we excuse my English teacher from my riding lessons? He isn't needed there, and the poor man seems so tired!

I'll consider it. What else?

18

20

Well, I've been here for almost two months already, and I hardly know anything about your business. Would you be willing to show me around your offices?

Hm!

It might be a little premature. The world of business is extremely complex. But since I'd like you to play a role here one day, I suppose a glimpse can't hurt.

...our firm ships raw materials and manufactured goods between consortiums and major industrial cartels worldwide. We need to be able to communicate directly with all of our clients and suppliers, at all times. This is the telegraph room...

DRRRING DRRRING DRRRING DRRRRI DRRRING DRRRRING

...THE TELEPHONE HALL...

IT'S ... GIGANTIC!

19

21

Unbelievable!

I built it all from scratch, starting with a little warehouse I set up in the port...

...when I arrived in this country, thirty years ago.

Today, the old warehouse is a cafeteria for my sixty-fifth team of delivery men.

That's amazing!

Things always move fast here!

A few days later...

I'm proud of you, Karl. You did a good job on this English assignment. Hurry and get dressed for dinner. I'd like you to meet two of my friends.

Mr. Pollunder... Mr. Green... My nephew, Karl.

Pleased to meet you.

Over dinner, the conversation turns to business, a subject Karl knows nothing about.

As the meal winds down, Pollunder begins to take an interest in him, congratulating him on his English, asking about his impressions of America and inquiring into his background...

20

22

You should come out and visit me at my country house! My daughter, Clara, would be delighted to meet you.

I would be very happy to come. If Uncle doesn't mind, of course.

Why not? I have no objection. It would do you good...

...once your schedule permits, of course.

Does that mean I can go soon?

We'll have to see.

But then the very next afternoon...

Mr. Rossman, your uncle wishes to see you in his office immediately.

Come, Karl.

Mr. Pollunder is here to take you to the country, as we discussed yesterday. Except I see you're not ready to leave.

But I... I didn't know we'd be going today.

If it's all too much trouble for you, we can put off the visit to another day.

It's no trouble at all! I have plenty of time! In fact, I even made a point of leaving the office early today.

21

You'll miss your riding lesson. Have you cancelled?

No, I didn't know I was supposed to...

And Mr. Mack?

He'll be fine without me. Besides, he goes every day.

Oh, come on, one time won't hurt! Besides, my daughter is already expecting Karl. She can't wait to meet him!

Well, in that case... But he'll have to be back in time for his English lesson.

Oh, dear! One evening and one night—that's not much, is it?

Well, it's that or nothing.

Understood. I'll bring him back tomorrow morning, first thing.

He isn't saying anything... Maybe he has no other objections?

And so Karl runs to his room to get ready.

Did he leave? I hope he wasn't angry...

Of course not!

On the contrary, your uncle is thrilled I invited you!

22

24

If he seemed a bit reluctant, it was only as a matter of principle...

He takes your education very much to heart, you know...

With traffic tied up by a demonstration of striking metal workers, the car has to take side streets to get out of town.

WORKERS UNITE!

METAL WO ON STRIK

Not wanting to miss a moment of all the goings on and excited by the prospect of the visit ahead, Karl tries to fight off his drowsiness...

23

Chapter 3:
AN ESTATE OUTSIDE NEW YORK

Here we are.

HUH? What? ... Oh! I'm sorry. I must have drifted off for a moment...

Ah! Mr. Jacob! Finally!

Rossmann. My name is Karl Rossmann. Jacob is my uncle's name.

Yes, of course...

And you must be Miss Clara.

We have another guest.

Who?

Mr. Green. He turned up unannounced.

Well, he couldn't have come at a worse time! Why tonight of all nights? What's the point of living far from New York if we can't have some privacy!

Perhaps he won't stay long...

That would surprise me. He has some important business to discuss with Papa. I'm sure they'll be up well into the night.

But we won't let it spoil the evening. After dinner, I'll give you a tour of the house. I have a piano in my room. You can play something for me. I hear you're very talented...

24

Come in, come in! Dinner is ready! We've been waiting for you!

What an ass!

I'm surprised Karl had permission to come. His uncle keeps such a close eye on him!

Why doesn't he mind his own business?

Soon Green has Pollunder talking shop with no further regard for Karl, who starts to wonder whether he should have come at all.

I actually hadn't planned to drive out here...

...but when I stopped by the office to see you this afternoon, you were already gone...

SLURP

I'm afraid that's my fault. I'm the reason Mr. Pollunder left the office early. Please accept my excuses. I'm terribly sorry.

25

28

Oh, that's all right, no need to apologize! After all, here I am, enjoying my dinner in charming company. What more could an old bachelor want!

The meal drags on, becoming increasingly unpleasant for Karl.

Be patient! As soon as we leave the table, we'll be alone, you and me....

Our young man doesn't have much of an appetite, does he? Wait till I tell his uncle that he insulted Miss Clara by snubbing her dinner!

See how sad she looks...

Hee hee!

When dinner is over, Karl withdraws to the side of the room.

I really can't stand that man...

...first he invites himself over, then he acts like he owns the place. And why is he playing games with me? What have I done to him?

And Clara... She really is very beautiful, but I don't like her manners any more than his...

As for Mr. Pollunder, I don't understand his attitude. He seemed so glad to welcome me at first, and then he spent the whole meal staring at his plate as though I wasn't there!

26

I'm beginning to see why my uncle had misgivings.

Maybe it's not too late to go back tonight...

If the chauffeur is off duty, there's nothing to stop me from walking home...

I'd be back at my uncle's first thing in the morning. I could surprise him the moment he wakes up, maybe even have breakfast with him...

You don't seem very happy to be here!

Follow me! We'll try to save what's left of the evening...

Are you coming or not?

Isn't there any electricity in this part of the house?

Not yet. We only just moved into this old ruin, so the renovations aren't quite complete.

I didn't know there were old houses in America too...

Of course there are! Hee hee!

27

Here, this is the room you'll sleep in tonight.

Not so fast!

I just want to have a look!

Later. For now, you're coming with me!

I said: COME!

If she thinks she can boss me around, she can think again. It's not like I'm some kind of lapdog!

HEY!

You almost pushed me out the WINDOW!

If you don't start behaving, that's exactly what's going to happen to you!

28

Karl breaks free from Clara and grabs her in turn.

Aaaaa

Why is she moaning like that? I'm not even holding her tight...

You're HURTING me! If you let me go, I'll show you something you'll like...

No thanks!

WHOAA! ...

?!

Poor baby! Didn't see that coming, did you?

You're out of your mind! Let me go!

So that's how you treat a lady, is it? You deserve a proper slapping! And if I wasn't holding myself back, I'd give it to you! It's a pity, really. You're such a pretty boy. Nice and sturdy, too. If you knew a bit of jiu jitsu, you'd have had the upper hand.

Why didn't you want to come to my room, anyway? Don't you like me?

LET ME GO!

29

32

I can't decide which would be more humiliating: a slap or a pardon? I suppose I'll let you go. Hopefully you've learned your lesson.

I wonder what Mack will say when I tell him about this...

Mack?

When is she finally going to leave?

Finished sulking yet?

Well, I'll be going then. If you change your mind, you can always come join me in my room. It's the fourth door to the right. Remember, you promised to play the piano for me...

And don't worry, I won't tell my father what happened. Good night.

Here's what I'll do: I'll go back down to Mr. Pollunder, tell him everything, and ask for permission to leave... Is this any way to treat a guest?

30

33

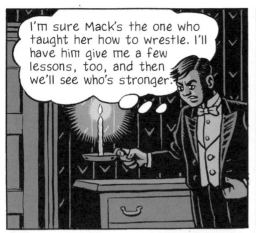

I'm sure Mack's the one who taught her how to wrestle. I'll have him give me a few lessons, too, and then we'll see who's stronger.

There's nobody...

I need to find the dining room, Mr. Pollunder, and my hat...

Already 11 o'clock...

I don't even know what floor we're on...

So many doors, so many empty rooms... What a waste! When you think of all those families living in a single room!

This isn't a home, it's a fortress!

That draft... There seems to be a large empty space over here...

I don't re-member having come this way.

MY CANDLE!!

SAVED! I see someone...

31

Who are you?

I'm Mr. Pollunder's guest and I'm looking for the dining room.

Follow me!

It's surprising how drafty this house is.

Yes, the renovations are far from done. And since the construction workers are on strike...

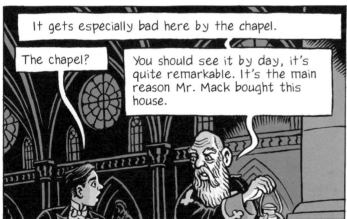

It gets especially bad here by the chapel.

The chapel?

You should see it by day, it's quite remarkable. It's the main reason Mr. Mack bought this house.

Mr. Mack? I thought the house belongs to Mr. Pollunder?

It does, but Mr. Mack closed the deal. Do you know him?

Yes, but I didn't realize he was connected to the Pollunders.

He is Miss Clara's fiancé.

!?!
...

This way. If you like, I can wait here to lead you back to your room.

Thank you, but that won't be necessary. Although...come to think of it, I probably will need you later.

32

Where has my hat gone?

Ah, Karl!

Isn't Clara with you?

She...uh... she's in her room. Mr. Pollunder, I have a favour to ask you.

Of course, you're my guest—ask away! Isn't it wonderful here in the country, in this house?

I...

Please, Mr. Pollunder, don't take this the wrong way, but I... I would like to go back home tonight.

Tonight??

As you know, my uncle did not give his consent wholeheartedly. I'm sure it's not because of you, since you're his best friend, but he must have his reasons. I shouldn't have insisted.

He has taken me under his wing and I owe him everything. I would be lost without his support. The poor schooling I received in Europe is hardly enough to secure a decent position here, or even the means to get by. And so to make amends for having acted against his wishes, I really need to get back as soon as possible.

33

Don't think I'm trying to keep you against your will, but unfortunately the chauffeur has left with the car and the telephone isn't hooked up yet.

I could walk you to the train, but the station is several hours away by foot. You wouldn't be home before morning.

Still, I'd rather take the train. But you mustn't come along. Your servant can show me the way.

I just need to find my hat first. I've looked everywhere.

Would this cap do the job?

Huh..? B... but isn't it yours?

No. You can have it, it's brand new.

?!?

It fits me perfectly.

As it should...

Now go back upstairs and say goodbye to Miss Clara.

Yes, please do...

Either way, I've been asked to pass on a message to you, but not before midnight.

A message? For me?

34

It's twenty past eleven. Go see Miss Clara and be back here in exactly forty minutes.

If it were up to me, I'd rather not...

Late, aren't you? I was just going to bed.

I can leave if you like. Anyhow, I wasn't planning to stay long.

No, no! Now that you're here, I want you to play that little tune you promised me. It would be a real pleasure—we hear so little music here.

Shall I wait for you in the hallway?

What time is it?

Eleven forty, sir.

The time is passing so slowly...

N... No, don't wait for me. Just leave the lantern, I'll find the way on my own.

So how about some music?

Of course...

PLINK

PLINK

PLONK

PLONK

PLINK

35

Karl rushes through the piece, eager to be done.

I'm really no good...

Bravo, Rossmann! I see you're not just a natural horseman, but a talented musician, too!

... Mack?

CLAP
CLAP
CLAP

Delighted to hear you tickling the ivories! Though, I can put up with just about anything if I have to. I've got a very open mind...

If I had known you were listening, I wouldn't have played. It was your... uh...f... friend...

Yes, I know. That's why I had her lure you over here. But why not stay with us for a moment? Come, have a seat...

DONG DONG DONG DONG DONG DONG DONG DONG DONG DONG DONGD

I...

I really have to be going... Good night!

What's the hurry?

36

39

Now where did he leave that lantern? I specifically asked him to...

!?

Forgot our agreement?

What took you so long?

Couldn't leave Miss Clara alone?

I can't answer all those questions at once!

Anyway, it doesn't matter. I was tasked with bringing you this letter. Here.

It's from my uncle. I thought it might be!

I don't care what you thought. Just read it. I've got other things to do.

JACOB&CO
NEW YORK

My dear nephew,
As you know, I am a man of principles. While this may be a burden to those around me as well as myself, it is to my principles that I owe everything I am, and I have no intention of abandoning em now. That is today. That is

them now. That is why, after today's incident, I have no choice but to send you away.

37

Don't try to contact me. Any attempt to do so would be futile. You decided against my will to leave me this evening, and you will have to assume the consequences for the rest of your life.

I have chosen as my messenger my fait[hf]ul fri[end] Mr. Green. No doubt he is [bett]er su[...] I to offer you soothing wo[rds] an[d] [j]udicious advice as you [...] [...] path of independ[ence]

on [...]
As I try to [...] of what has happened [...] only say to myself once a[...] no good will ever come from your family, my dear Karl.
I wish you every succes[s] in your new life.
Your devoted uncle
Edward Jacob

Your uncle also asked me to give you this.

!?

My trunk! My umbrella! How...?

A certain Schubal, chief mechanic with the Hamburg-Amerika Line, found them on his ship. Lucky for you, there's still a few honest people around.

Fine. I think we're done. There's no reason for me to stay in this house, where I was only welcome as the nephew of my uncle.

I'll just ask you to show me the way out. I don't expect anything else from you.

Very well.

38

!?

Surprised to find himself suddenly in the open air...

...Karl considers which road to take.

Let's see... How do I get to New York?

WOAH!

WOAH! GRrrrrr

I think it was this way...

But rather than go back to New York, where nobody is awaiting him—and one person in particular most definitely is not—Karl strikes out in the opposite direction.

WOAH!

WOAH!

WOAH!

WOAH!

WOAH!

39

42

Der Marsch nach Ramses

Chapter 4:
THE ROAD TO RAMSES

In dem kleinen Wirtshaus, in das Karl nach kurzem Marsche und das eigentlich nur eine kleine letzte Station des Newyork Fuhrwerkverkehrs bildete und deshalb kaum für Nachtlager zu werden, verlangte Karl die billigste Bettstelle, die war, denn er glaubte mit dem Sparen gleich anfangen zu müssen wurde seiner Forderung entsprechend vom Wirt mit einem es sei er ein Angestellter, die Treppe hinaufgewiesen, wo ihn zerrauftes altes Frauenzimmer, ärgerlich über den gestörten empfieng und fast ohne ihn anzuhören mit ununterbrochenen Ermahnungen leise aufzutreten, in ein Zimmer führte, dessen nicht ohne ihn vorher mit einem Pst! angehaucht zu haben, sc Karl wußte zuerst nicht recht, ob die Fenstervorhänge bloß he ren oder ob vielleicht das Zimmer überhaupt keine Fenster finster war es; schließlich bemerkte er eine kleine verhängt ke, deren Tuch er wegzog, wodurch einiges Licht hereinkam s Zimmer hatte zwei Betten, die aber beide schon etzt waren. Karl sah dort zwei junge Leute, die in schwerem lafe dalagen und vor allem deshalb wenig vertrauenswürdi chienen, weil sie ohne verständlichen Grund angezogen schl eine hatte sogar seine Stiefel an.

em Augenblick, als Karl die Luke freigelegt hatte, hob einer läfer die Arme und Beine ein wenig in die Höhe, was einen d lick bot, daß Karl trotz seiner Sorgen in sich hineinlachte. ah bald ein, daß er, abgesehen davon, daß auch keine andere afgelegenheit, weder Kanapee noch Sopha, vorhanden war, em Schlafe werde kommen können, denn er durfte seinen er ergewonnenen Koffer und das Geld, das er bei sich trug, kei hr aussetzen. Weggehn aber wollte er auch nicht, denn er ge nicht, an der Zimmerfrau und dem Wirt vorüber das Haus w n zu verlassen. Schließlich war es ja hier doch vielleicht nic herer als auf der Landstraße.

I'm sure I'll find an inn before sunrise...

This should do. Anyway, I can't afford to be choosy.

ROOMS

I'd like to have your cheapest room, please.

Heck of a time to show up!

Well...here you are. Go in and keep it quiet.

Karl struggles to see in the dark for a few moments...only to discover that both beds are already taken.

?!

RRFFBLLI
ZZZZZ
RRRR

40

I wonder why they're sleeping with their clothes on... Maybe they work here at the inn.

I guess it would be safer not to sleep.

I'll check the contents of my trunk instead. With that Schubal, you never know...

What a mess!

It looks like everything's here: my passport, my money... With the bit I've got on me, I should be fine for a while...

Hey! Isn't that...

...THE CAP! The one that Mr. Green gave me... It was mine! I kept it in the suitcase during the entire voyage so it wouldn't get worn out...

And this smell? Oh, that's right...

sniff

It's the Veronese salami mother gave me before I left.

41

My poor parents... Will I ever see them again? I miss them so much! And to think I swore that I wouldn't write to them...

SOMEBODY THERE?

Uh... I'm sorry I woke you up. My name is Karl Rossmann and I'm a German.

Mmmm?

Since we'll be sharing this room, I'd like to ask you to tell me your names and nationalities. And just so you know: I have no intention of claiming your beds. You were here first, and besides, I don't intend to sleep tonight.

Don't let these fine clothes I'm wearing fool you. I'm poor and I...

All right, enough. My name is Delamarche and I'm French. This is Robinson, and he's an Irishman. Now shut up already, we want to sleep.

I've always been told you can't trust the Irish. It's funny— this one doesn't look so bad.... I'm more worried about the Frenchman.

RRRFBLZZz

To keep from falling asleep, Karl turns his attention to the picture of his parents.

Stay awake....

...stay awake...

...stay...

...awake...

ZZZZZz

42

The next morning, Karl gets better acquainted with his new companions.

HUH!? What?? What are you...

Tickletickle

HA HA!

They explain that they are unemployed mechanics, making their way on foot to the town of Butterford in search of work.

We don't have a penny left. We used up all our savings to pay for this room.

If you have nowhere to go, you can come with us. We'd help you with your trunk.

Nice suit... But not so great for finding work on a construction site.

If you like, we can sell it for you...

You can?

The innkeeper'll give us a good price.

I'm not sure I...

We'll be right back.

43

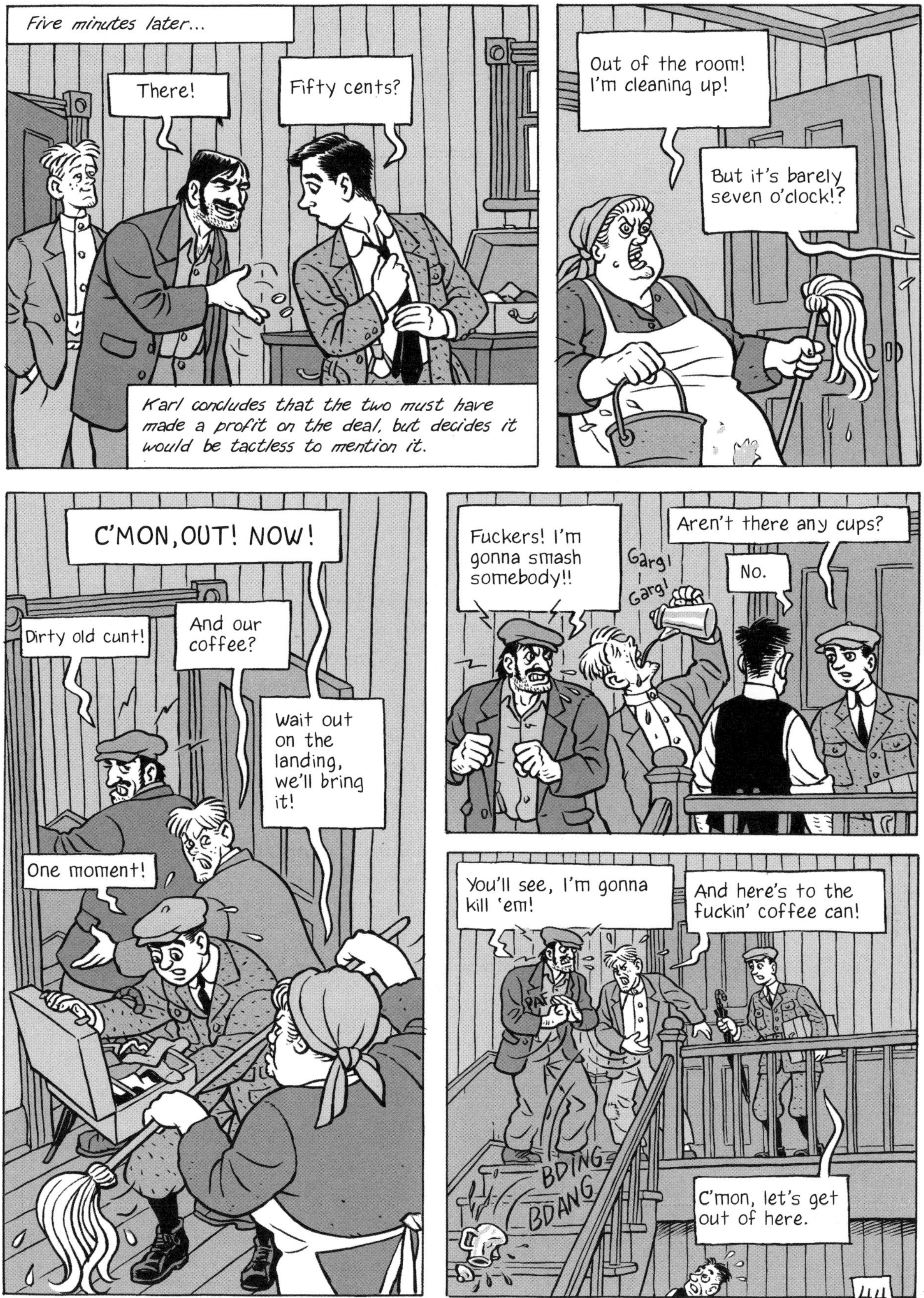
Five minutes later...
There!
Fifty cents?
Karl concludes that the two must have made a profit on the deal, but decides it would be tactless to mention it.
Out of the room! I'm cleaning up!
But it's barely seven o'clock!?
C'MON, OUT! NOW!
Dirty old cunt!
And our coffee?
Wait out on the landing, we'll bring it!
One moment!
Fuckers! I'm gonna smash somebody!!
Garg! Garg!
Aren't there any cups?
No.
You'll see, I'm gonna kill 'em!
PAF
And here's to the fuckin' coffee can!
BDING
BDANG
C'mon, let's get out of here.
44

Soon the road is jammed with vehicles carrying goods and workers to New York.

You men lookin' for work? Climb aboard! We're hiring!

JACOB

HIRING &

PFFFTTT!

GO TO HELL!

Those Jacob & Co. bastards, they're the biggest exploiters in the country! Goddamn scum!

pfft

JACOB & Co.

45

Troubled to think that he could have found himself working for his uncle, Karl is glad his companions turned down the offer.

Still... They could have been more polite about it!

How much further is Butterford?

Two days by foot.

Would one of you mind carrying my trunk for a while? It's getting a bit heavy...

♪

I SAID: WOULD ONE OF YOU MIND CARRYING MY TRUNK PLEASE! I CAN'T KEEP UP ANYMORE!

Bzzzbzzzbzzzt

Heh heh!

SURE, I'LL CARRY IT! HERE, HAND IT OVER!

Karl soon realizes that Robinson's generosity isn't entirely disinterested.

Hmmm... Not bad, thish shaushage...

Hey, leave some for me!

CHOMP CHOMP

I didn't even get a slice!

Buurp

Consider yourself lucky — your trunk just got a whole lot lighter.

46

51

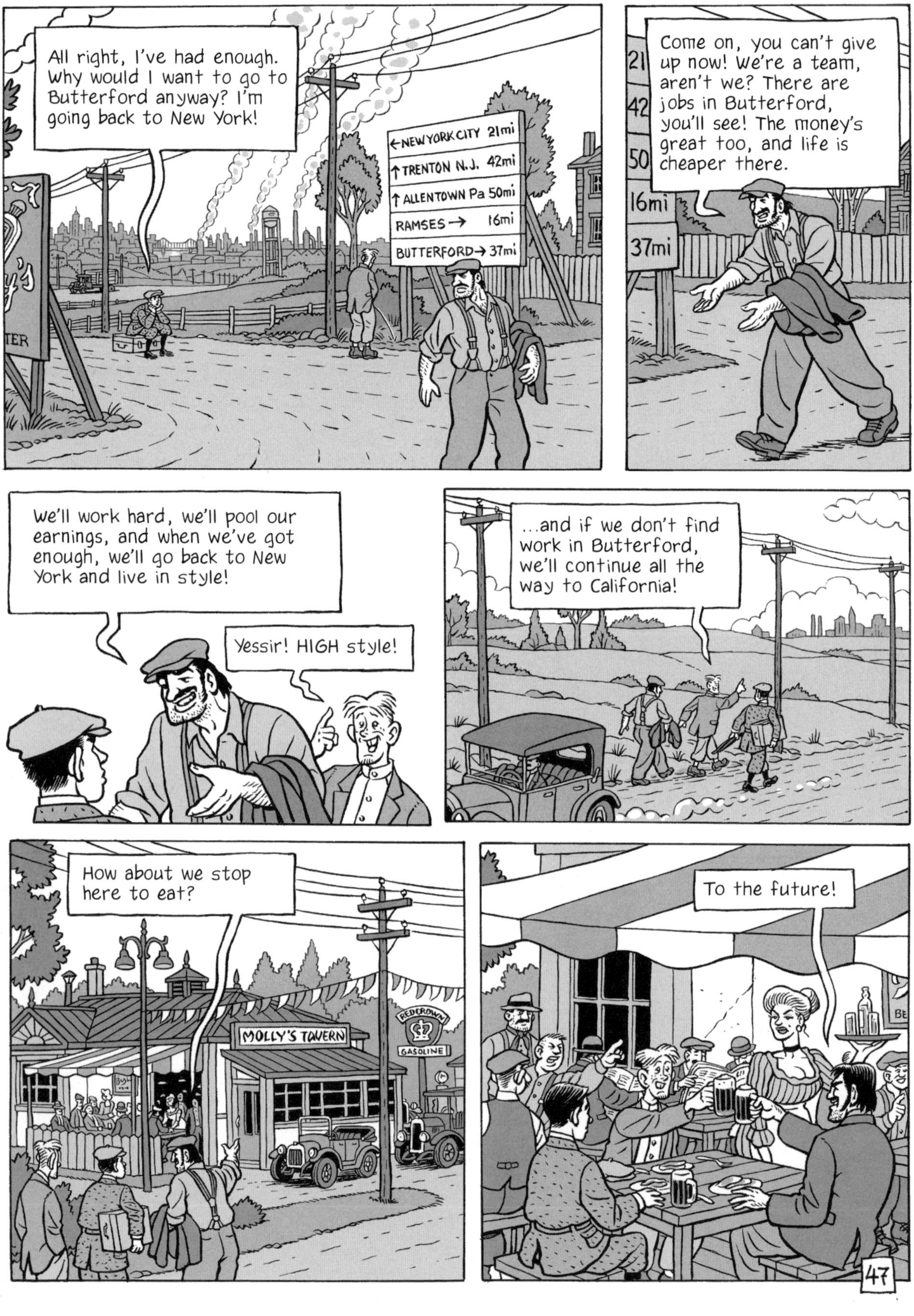
All right, I've had enough. Why would I want to go to Butterford anyway? I'm going back to New York!
←NEW YORK CITY 21mi
↑TRENTON N.J. 42mi
↑ALLENTOWN Pa 50mi
RAMSES → 16mi
BUTTERFORD → 37mi
Come on, you can't give up now! We're a team, aren't we? There are jobs in Butterford, you'll see! The money's great too, and life is cheaper there.
We'll work hard, we'll pool our earnings, and when we've got enough, we'll go back to New York and live in style!
Yessir! HIGH style!
...and if we don't find work in Butterford, we'll continue all the way to California!
How about we stop here to eat?
MOLLY'S TAVERN
GASOLINE
To the future!
47

Hey there, pretty lady! Wanna sit with us?

Cut that out! Who's paying?

He is!

Well, I guess that's normal. I've got to do my part... But they could have asked me first!

Annoyed at having to dip into his secret pocket and reveal his meagre savings, Karl tries to sort through his coins while his companions are distracted.

...thirty... forty... uh... how much is this one?

Paws off!

There, keep the change. My pleasure.

Thanks, you're a real prince!

KLLNG

Later...

We'll spend the night here.

Out in the open? How come? I can get us a hotel room.

No, no, keep your money. We'll be needing it.

48

53

Go fetch us something to eat instead. Hurry, we're hungry.

Uh... All right, fine. What would you like?

Bread, some bacon and beer...

Bread, bacon, and beer...

CHICKEN, MAYONNAISE AND FRIES!

THREE PLATES OF SAUSAGES! THREE!

FOUR BEERS!

TWO COFFEES, ONE TEA!

AHEM! Excuse me, I would like...

ONE TUNA SALAD!

Uh... bread, bacon and...

...beer.

49

How does anybody get served in this place? I'll never manage!

You look like you could use a hand, young man!

I'd like to order some food, but I don't know how...

Well, you've found the right person. I'm the head cook.

I'll take you to the storeroom. The food is fresher than here at the counter.

That's very kind of you, ma'am.

So, what'll it be?

Bread, bacon and beer. For three people.

Is that all? But that's prison food! Sure you don't want anything else?

No, no, thank you!

All right, as you like. Is it for here?

No. My two comrades are waiting for me outside, on the other side of the road.

Do you still have far to go?

Only to Butterford.

Why not spend the night here at the hotel? There's plenty of room.

50

It's just that... my friends... well, they're not very clean.

Then come on your own!

Thanks for the offer, but I'm afraid I can't accept.

You sure are difficult, aren't you!

How much do I owe you?

You can pay me later, when you bring back the basket. And if you change your mind, you're welcome to sleep here.

!?!

WAKE UP!! Thieves came and raided my trunk while you were sleeping!

Hmm?

HA HA HA!

HO HO HO!

?

51

We were starving, and when you didn't come back...

...we picked the lock to check for food. We didn't take anything, so you can just pack it all up again.

You sure took your sweet time, though! Didn't happen to eat at the hotel, did you?

GLUG GLUG GLUG

I know friends need to share, but this is too much! You can't just go through my things while I'm away!

I'm not going to Butterford with you, and I'm spending the night at the hotel!

Oh, is that right?

Hear that? What'd I say? Ya can't trust a kraut! Here we help him, we treat him like a friend, and he puts on airs, calls us thieves and then he ditches us the first chance he gets!

I trusted you and you broke open my trunk! And then instead of apologizing, you insult my people and try to humiliate me!

I've had it with both of you!

I better get away from here quick...

Careful what you say! We might run out of patience!

Robinson, I'm sure you know I'm right. I have nothing against you except that you let Delamarche give you orders!

52

Are you trying to cause trouble between us? Who the hell do you think you are? And how come you want to go to the hotel so badly?

I don't like this...

C'mon, tell me!

ANYBODY THERE?

Ah, here you are! I've looked all over for you! The head cook sent me to get the basket—she needs it right away!

Here it is.

She also told me to ask if you and your friends don't want to spend the night at the hotel after all. The invitation is still open.

Thank you, I will. But I...I'll be coming on my own. Give me a moment to gather up my things.

53

Hold on.... Where is the picture of my parents?

Haven't seen it.

If one of you has it, give it to me now and I won't hold this against you.

Please, it's all I have left of my parents. I'm very attached to it! It means more to me than anything else in that trunk!

Wasn't me.

I'll make a deal: if one of you has the photo, give it back right now and I won't make any trouble. Plus you can have whatever's in the suitcase!

Well, if that's how it is, I've got no choice: we'll have to search you.

If I find it, I promise that whoever has the photograph can have my suitcase. This is my last offer!

Have I gone too far?

54

There's no trace of your photo, sir.

For all I know, they've torn it up and thrown it to the wind...

Reluctantly, Karl gives up the search and follows the employee to the hotel.

THE OFFER STILL STANDS: BRING THE PHOTO TO THE HOTEL AND I'LL GIVE YOU MY SUITCASE! I WON'T TURN YOU IN! I PROMISE!

There's no reply, except for a stone rolling down the slope.

!?

POK

Probably just a coincidence... Or maybe a bad throw...

55

Chapter 5:
AT THE OCCIDENTAL HOTEL

ım Hotel occidental

'm Hotel wurde Karl gleich in eine Art Bureau geführt, in we
)berköchin ein Vormerkbuch in der Hand einer jungen
chreibmaschinistin einen Brief in die Schreibmaschine dikt
ußerst p... ...ren, der beherrschte und elastische Ta
gten an dem ... Wanduh
chon fast halb zwölf Uhr zeigte. "So!" sagte die Oberköchin, k
ormerkbuch zu, die Schreibmaschinistin sprang auf und stü
olzdeckel über die Maschine, ohne bei dieser mechanischen
ugen von Karl zu lassen. Sie sah noch wie ein Schulmädchen
chürze war sehr sorgfältig gebügelt, auf den Achseln z. B. gew
risur recht hoch und man staunte ein wenig wenn man nach
nzelnheiten ihr ernstes Gesicht sah. Nach Verbeugungen zu
e Oberköchin, dann gegen Karl entfernte sie sich und Karl sa
willkürlich die Oberköchin mit einem fragenden Blicke an."I
ıön, daß Sie nun doch gekommen sind", sagte die Oberköchin
ımeraden" "Ich habe sie nicht mitgenommen", sagte Karl. "Die
ırschieren wohl sehr früh aus", sagte die Oberköchin, wie um
che zu erklären. "Muß sie denn nicht denken, daß ich auch
marschiere?" fragte sich Karl und sagte deshalb, um jeden
zuschließen: "Wir sind in Unfrieden aus einander gegangen.
rköchin schien das als eine angenehme Nachricht aufzufass
d Sie also frei?" fragte sie. "Ja frei bin ich", sagte Karl und nic
wertloser. "Hören Sie, möchten Sie nicht hier im Hotel eine
ehmen?" fragte die Oberköchin. "Sehr gern", sagte Karl, "ich
etzlich wenig Kenntnisse. Ich kann z. B. nicht einmal auf de
reibmaschine schreiben. " "Das ist nicht das wichtigste", sagt
rköchin. "Sie bekämen eben vorläufig nur eine ganz kleine A
müßten dann zusehn, durch Fleiß und Aufmerksamkeit sich
ufzubringen. Jedenfalls aber glaube ich, daß es für Sie besse
ender wäre sich irgendwo festzusetzen statt so durch die We
meln. Dazu scheinen Sie mir nicht ...

CLAK CLAK CLAK CLAK CLAK CLAK BING♪ CLAK CLAK CLAK CLAK CLAK CLAK CLAK CLAK CLAK

Ah! You've changed your mind! Come in!

CLAK

And your friends? Are they here too?

No. Actually, we, uh... we had a little disagreement.

Ma'am...

Will you still be needing me?

No, Therese, that'll be all for this evening. You can go.

Good night, ma'am. Good night, sir.

Good night, Therese.

You were saying you've left your companions. In other words, you're free... How would you like to work here at the Occidental Hotel?

56

I'd like to very much, except...I've got no skills.

That's no problem, you'll learn as you go. How old are you?

I'll be sixteen next month.

Goodness! I thought you were at least seventeen!

You look like a sturdy, clever and resourceful young man. You'll have to start at the bottom of the ladder, of course, but that's better than being out on the road! With a little perseverance, you'll quickly climb your way up. Maybe you could be an elevator boy, for instance?

Yes, perhaps... But you're being so helpful, and I haven't even introduced myself! Please excuse me. My name is Karl Rossmann.

Sind sie Deutscher?

Yes, I'm German. From Prague, in Bohemia.

Is that so?! What a coincidence! I'm from Vienna, which is right nearby! My name is Grete Mitzelbach.

Wien

Praha

I know Prague very well. I worked in Wenceslas Square, years ago.

Now that I know you're a fellow country-man, I can't let you walk away again! So tell me: how would you like to be an elevator boy?

Actually, I think I'd like it very much!

Wonderful! You'll see—you'll enjoy it here.

We could talk about home for hours, but you must be dead tired. Come, I'll show you to your room.

57

It's on the eighth floor. We'll take the elevator.

Sleeping, again!

But let's not wake him up. Poor boy—he works twelve hours a day, and as you can see, he's not too sturdy...

SSSNRRZZZZZ

But it's a question of time. Six months at this rate and he'll be fine. And in a few years, he'll be strong as an ox.

That's America for you!

If you had come with your friends, you would have slept in the employee dormitory, but since you're alone, I've had the little sitting room by my bedroom made up for you for tonight.

You'll be fine on the sofa. There's no sink, but in case you want to wash, I've ordered up hot water and everything you need. I'll lock the door, so just make yourself at home.

58

65

Is everything satisfactory?

Yes, ma'am, I'm infinitely grateful. Uh... my former companions might stop by tomorrow with something that belongs to me. If they do, could you ask for it to be brought up?

Of course.

Oh, and one last thing....

THERESE?

Yes, Ma'am?

When you come to wake me tomorrow morning, please use the corridor so you don't bother our guest.

Yes, ma'am.

I sleep poorly and I start work at five-thirty in the morning, so Therese has to come wake me up.

I'll let you get some rest now. Good night, Karl.

Good night, ma'am. And thank you again for all your kindness.

KNOCK
KNOCK
KNOCK

One moment!

59

66

It's Therese. May I come in?

Well, I... I'm not dressed, and I was about to go to bed. Give me a minute to put my clothes back on.

There's no need. Unlock the door. I'll wait a moment so you can get under the covers.

Uh... All right.

There, you can come in now.

I won't stay long. I just wanted to talk a bit. Uh... I don't see a chair.... May I sit on the sofa?

Yes, sure...

So, you've decided to stay at the hotel?

I think so, yes.

That would be nice, because I have no one to speak with. I feel so alone here!

But what about the head cook?

Oh, she's very kind to me, but she's not like a friend I can really talk to, heart to heart. After all, she is my boss.

I owe her everything. I'm very lucky that she hired me to help her.

60

I started out in the hotel as a kitchen maid. It was hard work, and I was always afraid I'd be fired.

It was so difficult, I think it even stunted my growth. I'm already eighteen, but I don't look it...

The head cook noticed the way I folded napkins. I've always been very good at napkin folding.

She hired me as her secretary. And there's no end of work! You can't imagine all the letters that have to be written! And then there are the errands in town...

Tell me, what's the name of the town?

Ramses. Didn't you know? It's a city, actually. Not as big as New York, of course... If you like, you can come with me next time I go.

All right.

So, you were lucky after all...

Lucky? I suppose... Sometimes, though, I think the head cook only keeps me on out of pity!

I'm not a real secretary—I've never studied! I can hardly type! I even wondered—you can see how wicked I am—whether the head cook didn't hire you so she could replace me and send me back to the kitchen. It might not even be such a bad idea...

61

Absolutely not! I'll be an elevator boy, and you'll stay on as secretary!

Oh, Karl, you're so kind!

Please, don't tell the head cook about our talk! I'd die of shame if she found out!

I promise. It's our secret.

Life sure seems difficult here!

Boo hoo hoo!...

I think it's time you got some sleep. If you like, I can wake you up around eight o'clock tomorrow morning.

It sounds like waking people is your specialty.

Yes, there are some things I do very well...

I'm quite skilled at folding napkins, for example!

Good night, Karl.

Good night, Therese.

62

Karl is eager to get started the next day...

But this will never fit!

We'll adjust it...

Perrrfect!

Welcome, Karl. Giacomo will show you everything you need to know...

LISBARY

There are 31 elevators in the hotel. As you can see, it's quiet right now. But when it's busy, we can hardly keep up.

Here, this one's yours! And that's Rennel. You'll take turns operating the elevator.

Hello.

So how does it work?

It's easy. You just move this lever, that's all.

But...what about the machinery?

Oh, we never touch it.

63

70

Too bad...

There is one trick, though...

See this cable? You can give it a little tug to go down faster when you've got clients waiting below.

But it's not allowed, so don't tell anyone.

We do 12-hour shifts and we take turns working nights, with a 24 hour break on Saturdays between shift changes.

Isn't that hard?

You get used to it... Sometimes I manage to sleep standing up for a few seconds without anybody noticing.

Really...

Ah, Karl! I have some news...

I've made arrangements to get you a room. It's a bit complicated, but things should work out.

I appreciate the effort, but please don't bother. I don't want any special treatment. I'll sleep in the dorm with the others.

As you like. But I should warn you: the elevator boys' dormitory...

64

...is not a very restful place!

They could at least turn off the lights.

Karl learns the tricks of his new trade...

This way, ma'am.

Thank you, sir.

C'mon! Faster!

I forgot my perfume. Would you mind running up for it? Room 612, on the nightstand.

Immediately, ma'am.

65

What a day... I'm not sorry to see it end!

Rossmann?

I need to go to town. Mind filling in tonight? I'll make it up sometime.

All right.

Karl spends every free hour he can with Therese.

It's so kind of you to help me with these errands.

They get to know one another.

I'm the illegitimate child of a Pomeranian construction worker. Not long after I was born...

...my father left for America. Later, he sent for my mother and me to join him in New York.

66

We came to live with him. But he left for Canada soon after, and we never heard from him again.

I remember one winter evening, when I was five years old. We were walking—my mother and I, that is— through the city streets. The snow was whirling around us.

My mother was desperate. She was sick, penniless, jobless, homeless. I didn't understand at the time. I was so little.

You haven't experienced a New York winter yet! We wandered through the streets all night long, looking for shelter.

She said there was a construction site that might hire her. But she was worn out and worried that she wouldn't be strong enough to work.

We arrived at the site early in the morning. I sat down on a pile of bricks. Without saying a word, my mother climbed up the scaffolding, all the way to the very top of the building under construction.

67

And there, she walked straight ahead and plunged over the edge.

It's late. We should be getting back.

There are happier moments too.

Here, Karl, I have a present for you!

A business correspondence course!

If you study hard, you might be able to find a good job. I can help you if you like.

This is fabulous! Thanks, Therese.

Not easy to study under these conditions.

The weeks go by, sweetened by the prospect of a better life.

Sir, I hereby acknoledge

68

One day...

Hey, Rossmann! Guess what? I met a buddy of yours in town!

Delamarche, that's his name. Great guy. Even paid for my dinner this evening. He asked about you.

I know him, but he's not really a friend. Did he happen to mention a photograph?

A photo? No...

Then I don't want anything to do with him. You should be careful, too.

When Therese drops by later, Karl tells her about the incident.

From what you've told me about him, Delamarche sounds like nothing but trouble! Promise me you'll never speak to him again.

There's no need to worry.

Promise!

Fine, I promise: I'll avoid him if I can help it.

Not long after...

I need to step out for a moment. Can you keep an eye on my elevator?

No problem. Things are pretty quiet right now.

Let's go, faster!

Coming!

What kind of service is this?!

Finally, at three o'clock in the morning.

Phew! Things seem to have calmed down a bit. What an evening!

!?

Rossmann?

69

76

Chapter 6:
THE ROBINSON AFFAIR

Robinson!?! What are you doing here?

You've changed.

Things are looking up, my friend. How do you like my new vest? Not bad, huh?

Here, touch it!

Those aren't real pockets—they're just for show.

He reeks of liquor!

Heh heh!

Been drinking?

No, not so much....

You'll have to excuse me. I've got clients.

I hope he's gone by the time I get back!

But when he returns, Karl finds Robinson where he left him, only a bit more drunk.

Oh no!

CLACK

You really should drop by and visit us one of these days, Rossmann. You'll see! We're living in style!

Are you inviting me or did Delamarche send you?

70

Well...it's both of us...

All right, so you're going to tell him exactly what I'm telling you now: the two of you have caused me enough trouble. I don't ever want to see you again! Is that clear?

C'mon, buddy, you're killin' me already! I'm your friend...

Come and see us, we're living like royalty! We're staying with this FANTASTIC dame! An OPERA singer, if you can believe it!

♪♫ O MIO BABIIINO CAAROO ♪♫

Hey! Keep it down! This is a hotel!

All right, fine... but whatever you say, I'm still your friend!

Uh... Karl? Mind lending me a bit of money?

So you can drink some more? You look even worse than before!

Wh...? No...

I suppose Delamarche put you up to this, didn't he?

Fine, I'll give you some, on one condition: you get out right now and you never set foot here again. If you like, you can always write to me...

...Karl Rossmann, elevator boy, Occidental Hotel.

...So, want the money or not?

...Robinson?

Rossmann...

71

Rossmann... I... I don't feel well at all! ... I think I... I'm gonna... be siiick!

NO!! Not here! Get a hold of yourself!

Bbbeuheuheuaaargk!

Too late...

You're a real friend, Rossmann. I think I'm feeling better now...

Beuheuargk!

Karl feels a surge of panic as he considers the possible consequences of Robinson's actions.

Customers! I just hope they don't notice anything!

Coming!

72

People keep coming, and with every return trip to the lobby, Karl worries what he'll find down below.

At last! Let me deal with that lowlife now... Where is he?

Aaaah

There you are! C'mon on, let's go!

I couldn't if I wanted to. I can't even stand up!

Well, you can't just stay here!

I can't move! Let me die here, please— that's all I'm asking!!

Are you kidding me?

I'll have someone take you to the hospital.

NO! NO! NOT THE HOSPITAL!

I need to find a solution, and fast!

Can you fill in for a second?

No problem.

73

Now promise to be reasonable and try holding yourself up. I'm going to take you to my bed in the dormitory.

You're too good to me, Karl!

We just need to get there without attracting attention...

You're the only real friend I've got... Delamarche is always on my back! And that cow, Brunelda—I can't stand her!

What's he hurrying for?

Maybe you should get Rennell...

What'm I saying? Renell's not here, he's with Delamarche. They're the ones who sent me to fetch you.

A few more steps and we're there.

When they get to the dormitory, it's chaos as usual, and Karl finds another elevator boy sleeping in his bed.

ZZZ

I'll put you in Rennell's bed. If he finds you when he comes in, he'll know what to do.

SNRRZZZ

74

83

What a night!

What're you doing here? This is my elevator!

Rossmann!

Where did you disappear to?!? What's going on?!

I asked you to fill in for me, didn't I?

But that's not enough! You need to let management know! What do you think they put the phone in for?

I didn't know...

Well, right after you left, the guests from the 4:15 express train arrived! And of course I couldn't operate both elevators at the same time!

At exactly that moment, the manager passed by and saw the guests waiting for your elevator. He called me and asked where you were...

But since you didn't say where you were going, I told him I didn't know. So he called for somebody to fill in right away.

He seemed really furious!

75

But this is the first time I've ever left my post!

It was one time too many!

Maybe they won't fire you. You'll need to come up with a good excuse, though.

You're suppposed to report to the manager's office.

If I was you, I'd get there as fast as possible!

If they investigate and find Robinson, I'm done!

Actually, there's no rule that says you can't put up a drunk in the hotel dorm...

But then who'd bother to forbid the unimaginable?

L.ISBARY!

RULES

Ahem!

RULES

76

What do I do now? If I leave without being excused, it'll make a bad impression...

If they can't be bothered to notice me, maybe the incident doesn't matter to them either...

After all, I'm just an elevator boy—I'm totally insignificant. What harm can an elevator boy do?

And besides, the manager started out as an elevator boy himself. I'm sure he'll understand...

Rennell must be back by now. He'll have found Robinson and got him out of the hotel. That's all that matters. The rest will work itself out...

SO, WHO LEFT HIS POST WITHOUT PERMISSION?!?

I...

77

Do you know what this means? DISMISSED!

I... I didn't know that I had to call to report...

NO EXCUSES! I'm not interested in your lies!

Don't know the rules, is that it?

RULES

You wouldn't believe the trouble we had! Do you know WHO was waiting to go up after he left his post?

RULES

Not Judge Turnbull?!?

Himself! He was left stranded by the elevator for a full five minutes!

HEAVENS! That's terrible!

Actually, I know this rascal already. He's the only elevator boy who doesn't greet me when he goes by.

I'm sorry, sir, but I...

... I assure you that I do greet you. I'm from Europe, where people greet each other more than necessary and I haven't lost the habit. Of course, since I pass your lodge a hundred times a day, I don't do it systematically, but...

YOU NEED TO GREET ME EVERY TIME! NO EXCEPTIONS!

You've got to hold your cap in your hand when you talk to me, and you need to call me sir and maintain a polite tone! At all times! You want to remember that if you ever find another job!

78

And that's not all, sir. Because in addition to being rude, this delinquent is known to spend all his free nights on the town.

Mr. Head Porter must be making a mistake. I'm sure he has me confused with someone else....

EXCUSE ME?!! In thirty years, I've never got anyone confused. I'm not Head Porter for nothing!

The day I don't know who's who anymore, you might as well dismiss me on the spot!

What's the use of trying to explain with them? It's a lost cause...

Hello?

Hello, Grete?.... I haven't woken you up, I hope?... Oh, dear, my apologies... I'm sorry to have to bother you for such a trifle...

...but there's a young elevator boy here named...?

Karl Rossmann.

Uh... Karl Rothman...

I believe you've taken this boy under your wing. Yes, well, if you can believe it, he left his post without permission, and the situation caused us quite some trouble. I regret to say that I've had to dismiss him.... I'm sorry?... Yes, dismiss, that's right...

...No, it's no use arguing, my mind is made up... You know I'm always happy to oblige, but in this case... I'm afraid he doesn't deserve the interest you've taken in him... That's what happens when your trust is misplaced...

In fact, the head porter was just complaining about his insolence and bad manners. He also says that the boy spends all his nights on the town, living it up. Lord only knows where he gets the money...

That's going too far!

79

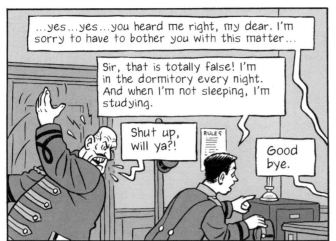

...yes...yes...you heard me right, my dear. I'm sorry to have to bother you with this matter...

Sir, that is totally false! I'm in the dormitory every night. And when I'm not sleeping, I'm studying.

Shut up, will ya?!

RULES

Good bye.

Let it be, Feodor. What the boy does at night doesn't concern us here. We're not going to waste our precious time investigating his comings and goings.

CLAK

The matter is settled. I'll sign this form for accounting, you'll get your pay and then you disappear. You can count yourself lucky. I wouldn't be doing this if it wasn't for the head cook.

RRRING

Hello? ...Is that you, Best?

...they did? ... where??

WHAT?!? That's outrageous! ... Unthinkable!... I want you here right away!

Feodor, don't let go of him yet.

CLAK

There have been new developments. The matter isn't as simple as we initially believed...

80

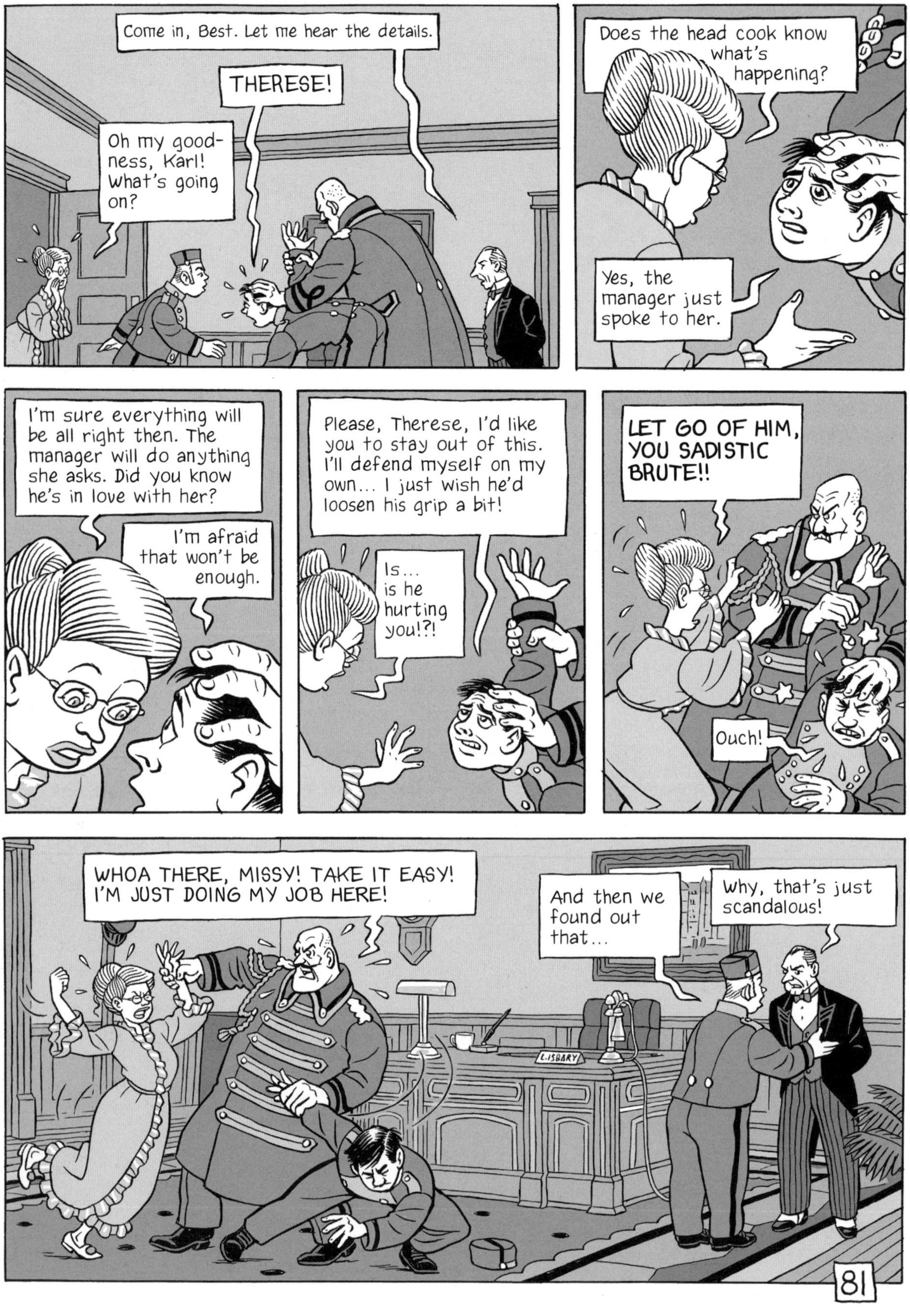
Come in, Best. Let me hear the details.
THERESE!
Oh my goodness, Karl! What's going on?
Does the head cook know what's happening?
Yes, the manager just spoke to her.
I'm sure everything will be all right then. The manager will do anything she asks. Did you know he's in love with her?
I'm afraid that won't be enough.
Please, Therese, I'd like you to stay out of this. I'll defend myself on my own... I just wish he'd loosen his grip a bit!
Is... is he hurting you!?!
LET GO OF HIM, YOU SADISTIC BRUTE!!
Ouch!
WHOA THERE, MISSY! TAKE IT EASY! I'M JUST DOING MY JOB HERE!
And then we found out that...
Why, that's just scandalous!
L. ISBARY
81

Ah, Grete, you've come after all! You really shouldn't trouble yourself over this good-for-nothing.

Wait till you hear what your protege has been up to! At this rate, he's not only going to wind up out of work but in jail, too!

I'd like a few words with him first.

And you! Let him go! He isn't a murderer after all!

Humph...

Don't worry, Karl, we'll work this out. I'm sure the manager would like to keep you as well. He's a good man, but you need to understand that his nerves are easily frayed. His work is very demanding...

Hm-hm! Let's come to the point! The head elevator boy, Best, is here to report what happened.

A short while ago in the dorm, we found a stranger sleeping in a bed, completely drunk. When we woke him up, he began making a racket and shouting that he was Karl Rossmann's guest.

82

We tried to calm him down. There was...uh...a bit of a fight.

Ouch!

LEMME GO!!

BOF

BAM

This bed belongs to Rossmann! You'll pay for this!

AH!

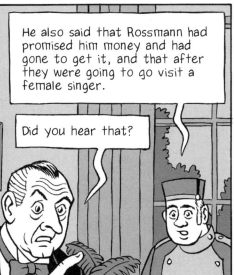

He also said that Rossmann had promised him money and had gone to get it, and that after they were going to go visit a female singer.

Did you hear that?

...

Well?

May I leave now, Sir? I have to get a doctor. The stranger needs medical attention.

Yes, go ahead.

Well? I'm still waiting... What do you have to say for yourself?

It's true: I do know that man. He's Irish and his name is Robinson. But he's not really a friend, no matter what he says...

I'm the one who brought him to the dorm. It was a mistake, I admit it, but I had no choice, since he was in no shape to leave on his own. That's all. The rest is just the ranting of a drunk man.

He said you promised him money. Is that true?

83

Yes, it is. I forgot to mention it. To get rid of him, I promised to give him my evening's tips.

Your story is full of contradictions. You're tripping over your own lies!

First, you tell us the man is Irish and that his name is Robinson. Whoever heard of an Irishman named Robinson? You also say he was too drunk to leave the hotel on his own...

...and yet he came in on his own two legs. That means you must have got him drunk while he was here. God only knows where you got the alcohol...

Lastly, you omit the fact that you promised him money. And when you're reminded of this crucial detail, you admit it, saying that you forgot to mention it, without explaining where exactly you intended to get this money.

You could be accused of theft.

Seeing no chance for a fair hearing, Karl falls back on his only remaining privilege: the right to remain silent.

Sniff

What's the point of defending myself if nobody's willing to listen?

RULES

Boo hoo hoo hoo hoo!

Won't you answer?

84

93

His silence is an admission.

I... I owe you an apology... I'm truly confused!

I promise, ma'am, that I've done nothing that could disgrace you. An impartial and serious investigation would prove it right away.

IMPARTIAL AND SERIOUS? You want to watch your words, boy!

sniff!

No, Karl, I'm sorry, but I've heard enough. As difficult as it is for me to accept this, and as much as I believe that you're a good boy at heart, there's nothing more to say. You see, even Therese is silent.

Boo hoo hoo!

She's not silent, she's crying!

I can't make sense of your behaviour, but I'm sure that an investigation would only incriminate you further. You can count yourself lucky that the manager is willing to let you go without pressing charges.

You always left your wages and tips with me. Where could you have found the money for your carousing?

To tell you the truth, I'd rather not know. Just let me help you.

I'm writing the Brenner Inn to recommend you. Go to them, rent a room for yourself, and I'll have your money and belongings sent over today.

85

94

I want you to know that I won't abandon you. I'll come see you at the inn tomorrow and we'll look at your situation together. You mustn't worry about your future.

Oh, Karl! I'm so glad that everything is working out after all!

Yes, yes, of course...

What's there to be glad about? I'm being dismissed as a thief!

Now get out! I have other things to do!

Excuse me, sir?

WHAT NOW?!

The man downstairs seems to be in pain, but he refuses to let himself be brought to a hospital. He says he wants to take a taxi home, and that Rossmann will pay for it.

Here, give him this. It's all I have.

He also wants you to join him in the taxi.

ABSOLUTELY NOT!

I believe there's nothing more to say.... Karl Rossmann, consider yourself dismissed from the Occidental Hotel.

86

Go find Best. Give him your uniform and leave this establishment immediately.

I want to see you walk past my lodge and out the door in fifteen seconds. **MOVE IT!**

Best? No, he's not here.

No idea...

Best? He's in the dorm.

Has anybody seen my pants?

A good five minutes have gone by before Karl finally reaches the hotel lobby.

87

YOU CALL THAT FIFTEEN SECONDS?

C'mere. I'm not done with you.

You can't tell me what to do. I've already been dismissed.

If you're here, you're not outside.

He's got a point...

WUMP

Anyway, there's nothing to worry about.

With all these people around, what can he do to me?

RRRRRRRRT

?!

88

You have no right to stop me!

No right, is that so?

My job, I'll have you know, is to anticipate the manager's every desire and handle any minor details that might escape his attention.

As the Head Porter, I am responsible not only for the main entrance of this hotel....

...but also for the three secondary entrances, the twelve auxiliary entrances and every single service entrance...

In fact, I have the power to prevent anyone I find suspicious from entering or leaving.

And you strike me as EXTREMELY suspicious!

Karl can't help but notice the foul smell emanating from the porter as he speaks.

I can yell.

And I can make you shut up... Besides, who do you think would step in to help you?

And I advise you not to try to slip out of a window. The windows are under my jurisdiction as well.

HEY?!? What're you doing?

I've got to search you. It's house policy.

And this is only because I forgot to greet you once or twice?

Not at all. I'm just doing my job.

89

With a powerful lunge, Karl manages to escape the porter's clutches.

HEY! YOU!

Grrrr

STOP HIM!

BDING

BDANG

Whew!

I need to get away from here fast!

Rossmann....

ROBINSON?!? What are you doing here?

I've waited a whole hour for you!

90

Chapter 7:
SAFE HAVEN

What did they do to you?

If you only knew... The BRUTES! Ah! I've paid dearly for this visit! I'm crippled for life!

Rossmann, Rossmann, I'm in TERRIBLE pain.

Must be his hair that's hurting.

He's hardly roughed up. The bandages were just a joke!

Ready to go? I don't have all day, you know!

Here.

Karl! Come with me...

??? ??? ?

VROOM

Well, I suppose I don't have anything better to do.

91

Is this really where you live?

All right, well, I'm done here then... Say hello to Delamarche for me.

Karl! KARL! You can't just leave! You don't even have a jacket!

So what? I'm sure I'll find another one somewhere...

Hold on!

92

You still owe me money.

How come? I already paid the fare!

There's a surcharge. I waited an hour for you in front of the hotel.

I'm sorry, but I gave you all I had!

Think you can just walk away? Who else is going to pay me, huh? WHO?

IT'S NOTHING, OFFICER! NOTHING AT ALL, I SWEAR!

Really?

That idiot!

What's going on here?

Sorry, officer, I...

ROSSMANN!

IS ROBINSON WITH YOU?

Right here!

HOLD ON, I'M COMING!

Delamarche will take care of everything, you'll see.

What a guy!

Well?

I'm dropping off Robinson. He's a bit beat up, but he'll get over it. I paid the taxi, except the driver wants extra. I don't have a penny left, so settle it with him and I'll get going.

Correction: I'll pay the driver, but you're staying here.

What do we owe you?

Golden Cab Co

94

Woof

HEY! HE'S TAKING OFF!

STOP!

Name?

Karl Rossmann.

...Rossmann... Papers?

I... I don't have them on me.

You've got no papers?

It's just...I lost my jacket and...

Is that so!... Address?

Uh... I'm currently looking for a room.

Got a job?

I had one until recently, but...

Dismissed from work?

You could say so...

When?

A... an hour ago.

Where from?

Afraid of being brought back to the hotel like a criminal by the police...

I said: where from?

Boo hoo

...Karl doesn't answer.

95

C'mon, speak up!

He was working at the Occidental Hotel.

He wasn't dismissed at all! He has a very good job at the hotel. He brought me back here because I'm injured.

NO! THAT'S NOT TRUE!!

This all makes no sense.... Do you know this individual?

I do, unfortunately. I gave him a hand once, and look at the thanks I get! The kid's an ungrateful little scamp, as you can see.

Indeed...

But you can leave him with me. I'll take care of him.

Sorry, sir, I can't do that. I need to bring him back to the Occidental Hotel to sort this all out.

Oh, I wouldn't bother if I were you. I can bring him back myself, if you...

HEY!

96

STOP!

PHWEE
PHWEE

POLICE! STOP THAT MAN!

WOUAH
WOUAH

Luckily for Karl, workers rarely side with the authorities.

Not knowing the area, he decides to run straight ahead, taking care to avoid the cross-streets.

531

Younger and more lightly dressed, he manages to outrun the police officer at first...

Daisy
SILK

97

But eventually fatigue sets in and his legs give way...

STOP HIM!

TRIII

!?

DELAMARCHE!?

Shh!

98

Hhhh

Hhhh

I'm fine..

whew!

You okay?

But how did you manage to find me?

I know these alleyways like the inside of my pockets. And I'm not a bad runner, if I say so myself! Nothing like a little police chase every now and then to keep you in shape.

Well, I've got to admit that I owe you one!

You better believe it!

If I hadn't been there, you would have been in big trouble...

Ha ha! Those kids! I had to give them a little shove when I ran by earlier...

EEEEK!!

MOMMY!

The taxi's gone....

And Robinson's inside.

I helped him up the stairs, sir.

Good boy.

Let's go! You're not just going to stand there, are you?

What've I got to lose?

99

It's so high...

Of course we don't have elevators like the hotel!

A bit tiring, isn't it? On the other hand, it's nice and quiet, and that's what really matters to Brunelda.

Besides, she never goes out.

You haven't met her yet. Well, you will soon. Just don't make any noise — Brunelda can't stand it!

Karl! There you are! I was sure Delamarche would bring you back!

Good old Delamarche! Never lets a buddy down! What would we do without him, huh?

She asleep?

I'm not sure... I thought I'd wait till you came back.

I'll check...

Hmmm... She's lying on the sofa, but I can't tell if she's sleeping. It's dark...

Is she sick?

100

What do you mean, *sick*?

He's never met her.

No, I bet he hasn't!

Hee hee hee!

Ha ha!

Hello. My name is Karl Rossmann, and I...

Heh heh

Hee hee

GET BACK INTO YOUR STINKING OLD RAT HOLE OR I'M GONNA CALL THE COPS!

Hee hee!

Nasty hags! I need to clear the trash out every now and then to get some peace around here!

And you, Rossmann, don't talk to just anybody! Watch yourself or you'll have to deal with me!

UNDERSTOOD?

Delamarche, is that you? What's all the noise?

Yes, it's me, dear. Can we come in?

Make it quick! I need you.

101

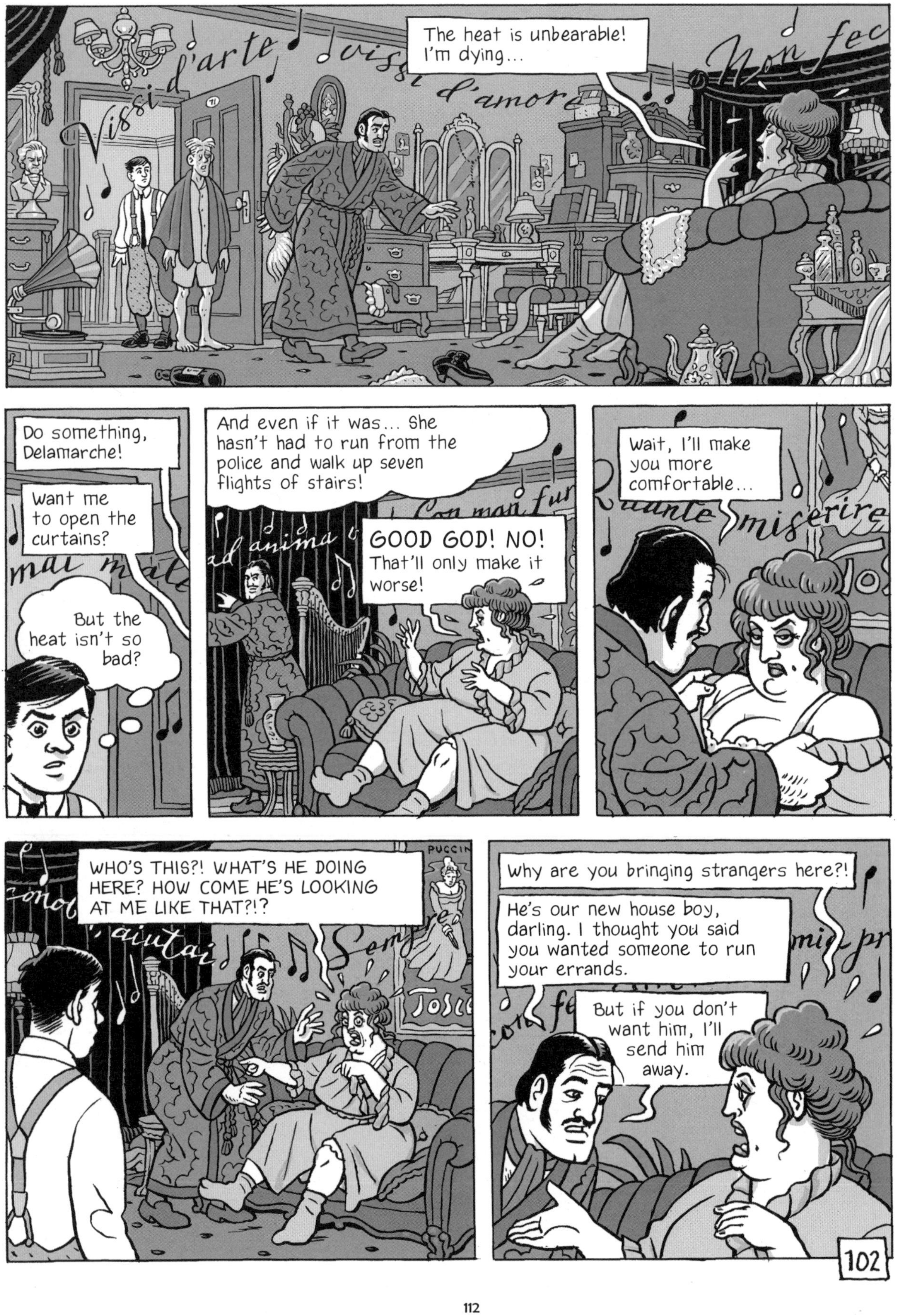

Vissi d'arte, vissi d'amore
Non fec
The heat is unbearable! I'm dying...
Do something, Delamarche!
Want me to open the curtains?
But the heat isn't so bad?
And even if it was... She hasn't had to run from the police and walk up seven flights of stairs!
GOOD GOD! NO! That'll only make it worse!
Wait, I'll make you more comfortable...
miserire
WHO'S THIS?! WHAT'S HE DOING HERE? HOW COME HE'S LOOKING AT ME LIKE THAT?!?
PUCCIN
Why are you bringing strangers here?!
He's our new house boy, darling. I thought you said you wanted someone to run your errands.
But if you don't want him, I'll send him away.
102

No, no, now that he's here, he might as well stay...

Thank you, ma'am, for letting me stay a bit. I've had a very difficult day and I'm terribly tired. If you don't mind, I'd like to lie down for a moment. I'll leave right after.

No, no, I want you to stay. But go ahead and have a nap. There's plenty of room.

Thank you, ma'am.

Hee hee!

Oh, Delamarche!

Finally, a bit of rest!

103

DELAMAAARCHE!

I'm too hot, I'm going to DIE! I need to take a bath RIGHT NOW! Send them away!

Get up, both of you! Onto the balcony!

??

Ouch!

HURRY UP, I CAN'T STAND IT! GET THEM OUT OF HERE BEFORE THEY DRIVE ME CRAZY!

Look at Robinson, wearing nothing but underwear in the presence of a lady! It's SHAMEFUL! And the other one has the eyes of a MADMAN! Have you seen the way he stares at me?

SEND THEM AWAY!

Yes dear.

LET'S GO, HURRY! And don't come back in until we say so!

It's always the same damn thing...

104

What a day!

ZZZ ZZZ

And to top it off, I've fallen into the hands of my worst enemy! What would Therese think!

Well, I'll have a quick nap and then I'll go.

Tomorrow's another day...

It's almost night when Karl wakes up.

Well, hello! Finally done sleeping, huh?

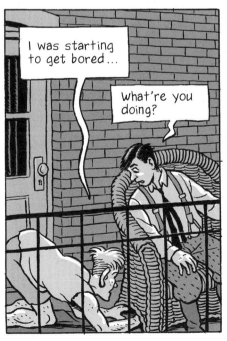

I was starting to get bored...

What're you doing?

Time for a little something to eat. Want some?

Uh... No thanks.

Ya gotta stash some grub if you don't want to die of hunger in this hellhole!

I don't understand why you put up with all this!

105

Ah well, you know, when people treat you like a dog long enough, you get used to it...

GLUG GLUG

Do you get sent out onto the balcony often?

Not all the time... It depends on Brunelda's moods. Sometimes it's because she wants to get dressed, or she wants to get undressed, or she's taking a bath... And sometimes it's for no reason at all...

One time, I dared to peek through the curtains... I swear, Delamarche made me regret it. See these bruises?

He didn't really want to hit me, but Brunelda made him do it.

She's got a good heart, though, even if it doesn't seem like it. You know, the other day I was alone out here on the balcony and I was so sad I started crying...

...well, she came out to comfort me! She wiped away my tears with the hem of her dress—her red dress, the one that looks so good on her...

...and the way she smelled! Ah, Karl! That perfume! I think I'll remember it forever!

And then? What hap-pened next?

106

Next? Well... Delamarche called her back inside, and I stayed on the balcony.

I don't understand why you stay. You could find work elsewhere.

It's not easy, you know...

Delamarche and me, we had a hell of a time after you ditched us, you can't imagine.

We decided we'd sing in the rich neighbourhoods to rustle up some food.

That's how we happened to see her coming home one day.

Gosh, she looked fine in that white dress...

107

...it was so tight, she needed a servant to help her up the front steps!

I don't know what came over me, but...

I touched her, just barely, with the tips of my fingers. I don't even know if she noticed.

But Delamarche sure did.

DIRTY BASTARD! THIS'LL TEACH YOU TO RESPECT A LADY!

CLAC

Brunelda was impressed.

Come here, you...

108

118

I waited by the door for hours. After a while, a servant came out to bring me a bowl of soup. It was compliments of Delamarche.

That was thoughtful of him...

The servant told me all about Brunelda—that she was a famous diva and a wealthy divorcee.

Her ex-husband, a cocoa manufacturer, was still mad about her. He'd come by when she was out to ask for her news, and he kept trying to arrange a meeting with her.

But the servant didn't want to pass on his messages anymore, because one time when he did, she flew into a terrible rage...

It even cost him a front tooth.

What a story!

Every word of it is true! I know her ex-husband. I've met him several times.

He used to arrange for me to meet him on the corner, and he'd give me a nice tip for news about Brunelda.

109

119

But then Delamarche found out and made me hand over the money. And Brunelda's ex doesn't come around much anymore...

Unbelievable... I wonder what he's after.

I dunno. But I know he'd pay a lot of money just to sleep out on the balcony like us.

...

That still doesn't explain how you three ended up here.

Well, first we went to live with Brunelda. But pretty soon, people began to talk, and she wanted to be left in peace.

So that's when Delamarche found this apartment. It's not luxurious, it's not very big, but at least there's nobody here to bother us.

And next door?

We avoid the neighbours as much as we can. There's a student, but we never speak to him. And then there's the women you saw this morning — they cook our meals for us....

110

And the servants? I suppose Brunelda must have had a few...

Oh, but there's not enough room for them here.

Besides, Brunelda dismissed them all on a whim one day.

GET THOSE MONKEYS OUT OF HERE!

All right, that's done.

So, what do we do now that we have no more servants?

There's Robinson.

Of course. Robinson, you'll wait on Brunelda now.

He's so sweet.

And that's how you ended up becoming their servant?

Oh, I wouldn't call it that... Most people don't know. I bet even you didn't notice.

But still, you do the work around here, right?

Yeah... But it could be worse.... Hardest of all was the move!

111

There's no elevator, so I had to carry everything up the stairs on my own.

Delamarche supervised.

You carried everything up ON YOUR OWN?! That must have been difficult!

Please, don't remind me! I think it ruined my health.

They say I'm not good for anything anymore, but it's just because I'm so tired all the time! I can't recuperate! I'm SICK, Karl! I'm going to DIE!

KOF
KOF
KOF

Oh, come on, you're exaggerating! I'm sure it's not that bad. A bit of rest and you'll be fine...

You said it, Karl! In fact, you're gonna replace me! And then I can recover.

The work isn't that difficult, you'll see. I'll show you what has to be done and I'll help you a bit at first. The complicated bit is putting order into all the chaos without moving anything. But whatever you do...

... don't bother Brunelda. When she's annoyed, she yells, and it's very bad for her.

112

Hmn. Sorry to disappoint you, Robinson, but I...uh...I've got other plans.

You don't really have a choice, do you? It's hard to get by out there, and where else will you find a job?

Plus you'd be paid! I'm a friend, so I just get a bit of pocket money. But you'd get a real salary. Here's your lucky break, buddy!

We needed somebody, and since we knew they had you slaving away at the Occidental Hotel, we thought of you!

It suddenly dawns on Karl that the night's events were all part of an elaborate setup to force him into Brunelda's service.

That's enough. I've made up my mind.

But...what're you doing?

I'm not staying here another minute! I don't know what I'll find elsewhere, but it's bound to be better than anything here!

No! Don't go in! It's off limits! They'll get angry!

If you want to obey them, that's your problem. I don't work for them, so don't try to stop me!

113

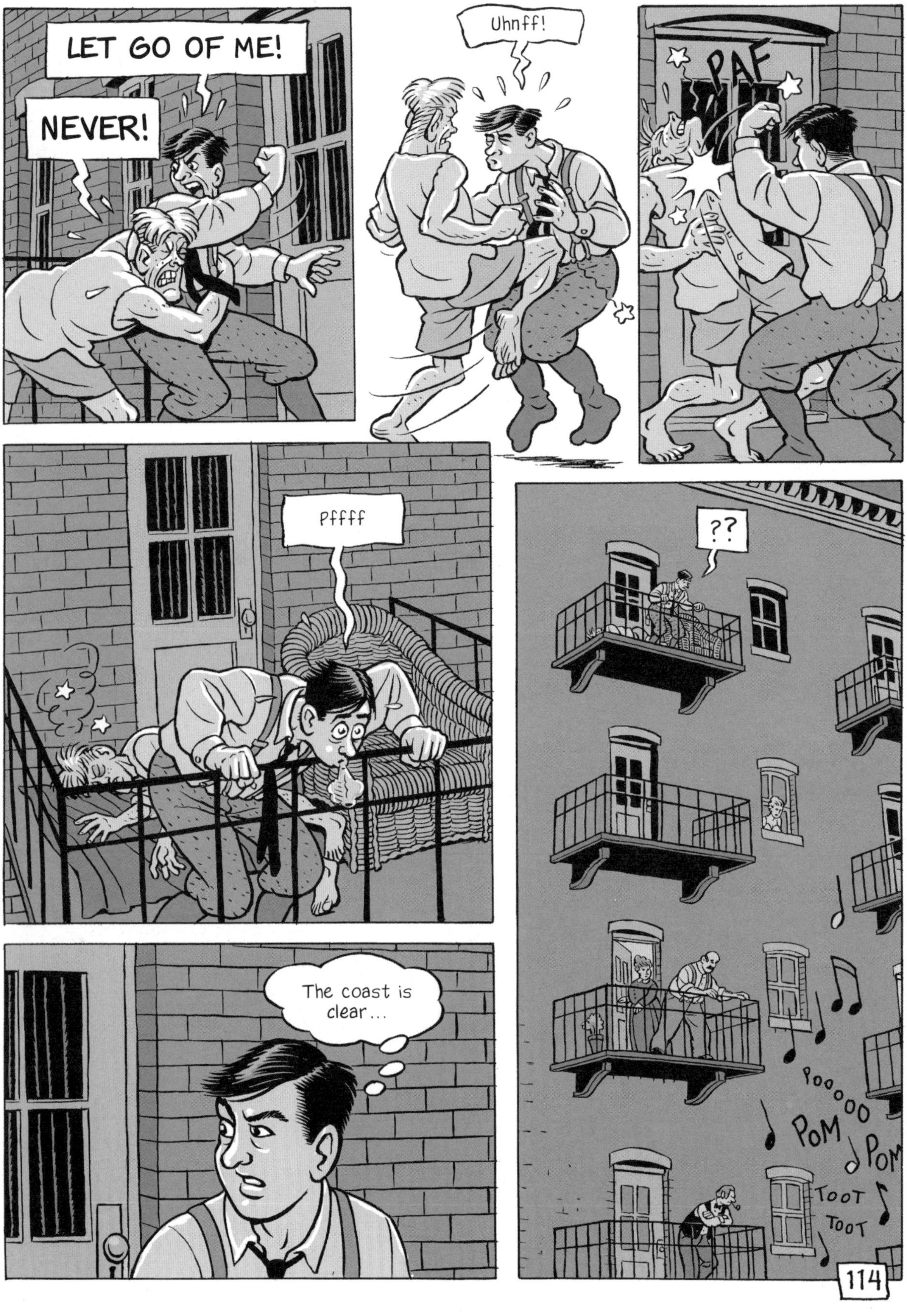
LET GO OF ME!
NEVER!
Uhnff!
PAF
Pffff
??
The coast is clear...
Pooooo
POM
POM
TOOT
TOOT
114

What's going on down there?

I don't know... A parade, maybe...

Probably a political rally or something like that...

115

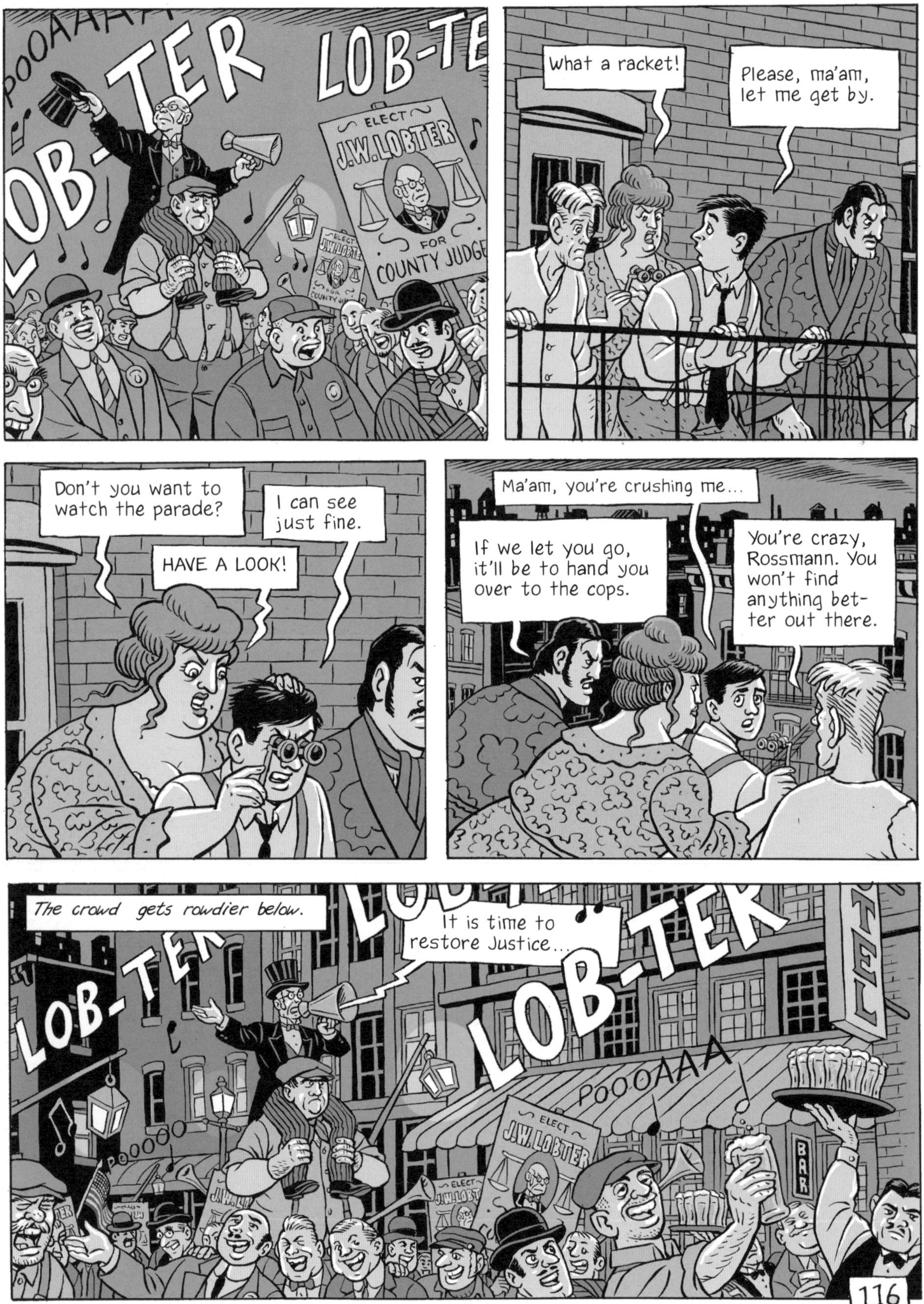
POOAAA
LOB-TER
LOB-TE
ELECT J.W. LOBTER FOR COUNTY JUDGE
What a racket!
Please, ma'am, let me get by.
Don't you want to watch the parade?
I can see just fine.
HAVE A LOOK!
Ma'am, you're crushing me...
If we let you go, it'll be to hand you over to the cops.
You're crazy, Rossmann. You won't find anything better out there.
The crowd gets rowdier below.
It is time to restore Justice...
LOB-TER
LOB-TER
POOOAAA
ELECT J.W. LOBTER
BAR
116

...Order and Decency in the district of...

Soon the candidate can barely make himself heard...

...especially after his opponents enter the fray.

Bunch of savages!

I've seen enough! I'm going to bed. Get the room ready for the night.

And hurry up!

Alright, here's my chance...

117

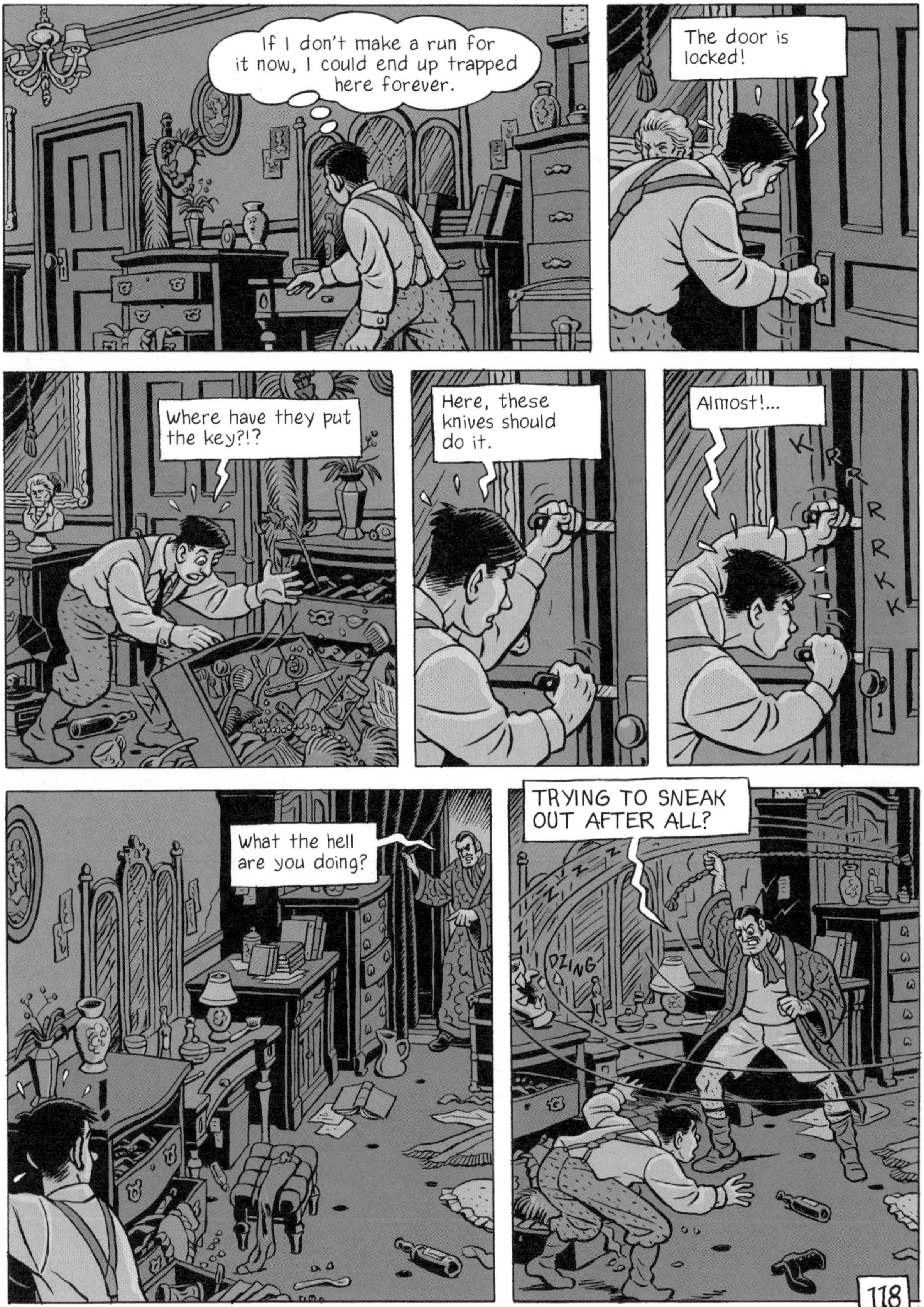
If I don't make a run for it now, I could end up trapped here forever.
The door is locked!
Where have they put the key?!?
Here, these knives should do it.
Almost!...
KRRRRKK
What the hell are you doing?
TRYING TO SNEAK OUT AFTER ALL?
ZZZZ
DZING
118

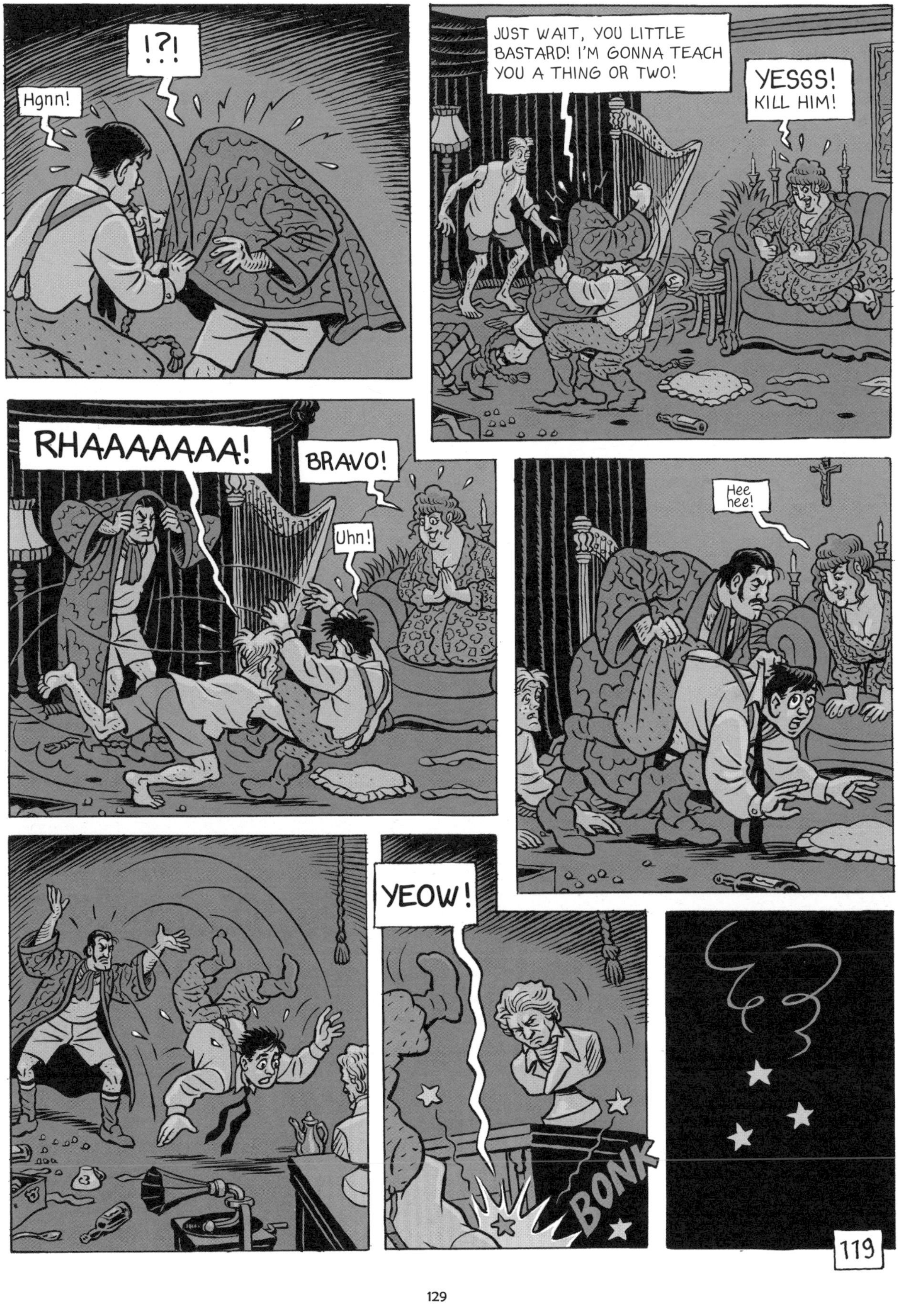
Hgnn!
!?!
JUST WAIT, YOU LITTLE BASTARD! I'M GONNA TEACH YOU A THING OR TWO!
YESSS! KILL HIM!
RHAAAAAAA!
BRAVO!
Uhn!
Hee hee!
YEOW!
BONK
119

When Karl finally comes to, the apartment is quiet.

Owww, my head...

What's this? Blood?!

Naturally they put Robinson in front of the door to keep me from leaving...

RRRFBLLLZZZ

I need some air!

120

130

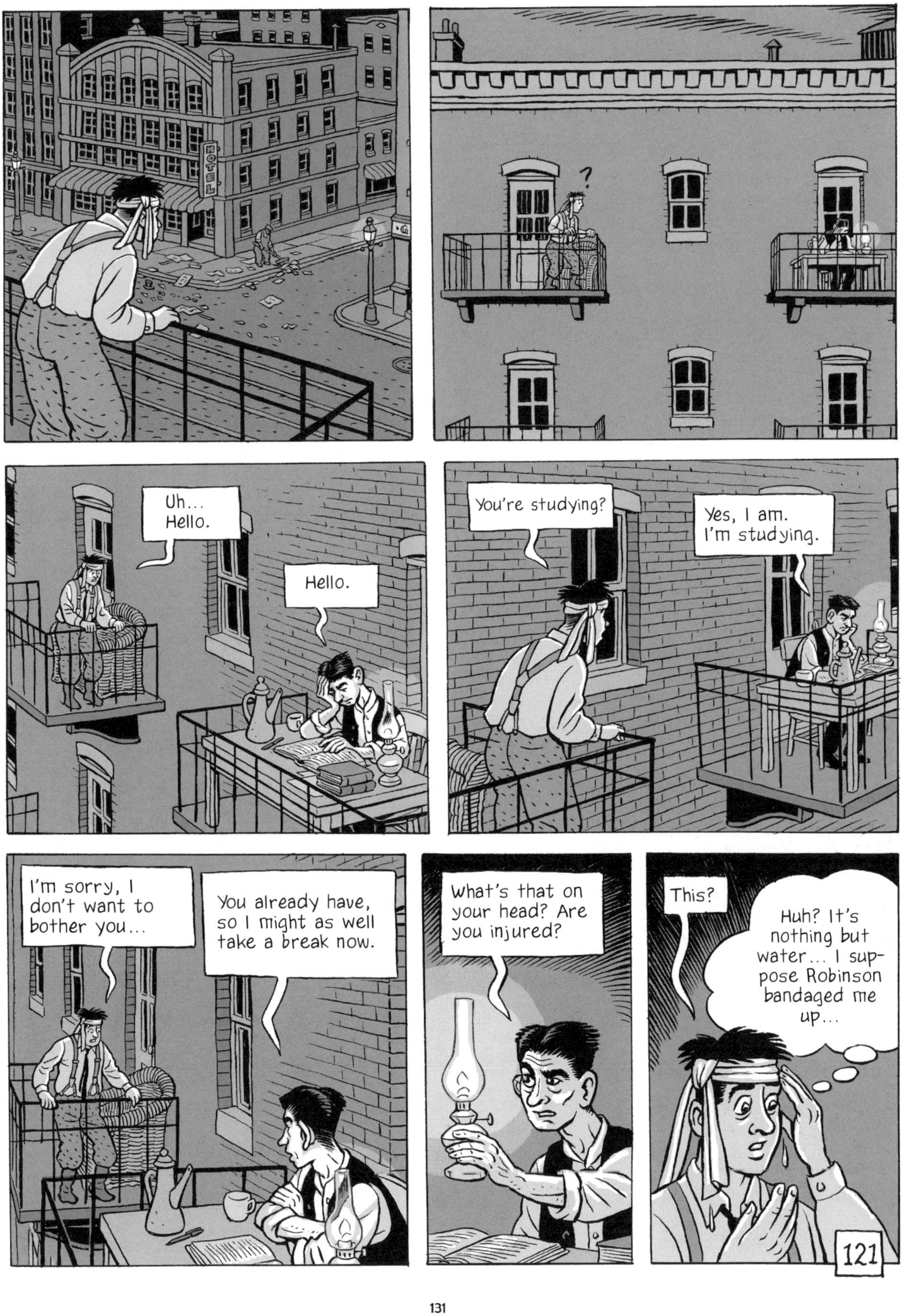
?
Uh... Hello.
Hello.
You're studying?
Yes, I am. I'm studying.
I'm sorry, I don't want to bother you...
You already have, so I might as well take a break now.
What's that on your head? Are you injured?
This?
Huh? It's nothing but water... I suppose Robinson bandaged me up...
121

Oh, it's just a bump. I... I got into a bit of a fight earlier...

Ah, so that's what all the noise was about. What happened?

You can tell me everything. Those people aren't exactly my friends...

Well, they want to force me to be their servant but I don't want to, so I tried to leave. Delamarche wouldn't let me and we got into it.

But why do you want to leave? Do you have another job elsewhere?

No, but staying here is out of the question. I know Delamarche, he's a real crook.

So what? You can't expect to choose your employers...

Take me, for instance. During the day I work as a clerk in a department store. The manager's a scoundrel and the pay is poor. But I still consider myself lucky to have a job.

You work during the day and study at night? When do you find time to sleep?

122

I'll sleep when I've finished my studies. In the meantime, I drink lots of black coffee — it does the trick. It's a real blessing. Want some?

No thanks, I don't like black coffee.

Me neither.

?

Will you be done soon?

It's all very slow. If things go well, I'll graduate next year. Or in two years... Maybe three.

I studied business correspondence for a while. Before that, in Europe, I wanted to become an engineer.

Don't even bother. School is a waste of time. It'll get you nowhere.

If I had to choose between university and my job at Montly's, I wouldn't hesitate for an instant.

Really?! So how come you're still studying?

I started, so I'll see it through.

I've got to admit, I don't understand why you would.

Did you see that man Lobter earlier? The one who's running for the position of district judge? I know him. He's an honest and competent man who'd do well in that position.

I don't really follow politics...

He's running a solid campaign and he has sunk all his savings into it. But...

123

133

...he's doomed to fail. Everybody knows it, himself included. But he hasn't given up. That's just how things are.

So, you think I should stay on as a servant?

Absolutely.

Now, if you don't mind, I'd like to get back to my work.

I'll stop bothering you. Good night.

Good night.

124

Maybe he's right...

Even though he dislikes the three of them, he thinks I should stay. And he doesn't even know that the police are after me...

After all, I wouldn't be here forever. One day, with a bit of luck, I'll find a real job, in a real office...

I'll be disciplined, I'll work hard, and I'll become a model employee...

My boss will have nothing but praise for me...

125

Chapter 8:
BRUNELDA

Auf! Auf! " rief Robinson, kaum daß Karl früh die Augen öff
Der Türvorhang war noch nicht weggezogen, aber man merk
an dem durch die Lücken einfallenden gleichmäßigen Sonne
wie spät am Vormittag es schon war. Robinson lief eilfertig m
esorgten Blicken hin und her, bald trug er ein Handtuch, ba
Wasserkübel, bald Wäsche-und Kleidungsstücke und immer w
n Karl vorüberkam, suchte er ihn durch Kopfnicken zum A
ufzumuntern und zeigte durch Hochheben dessen was er ge
er Hand hielt, wie er sich heute noch zum letzten mal für Ka
er natürlich am ersten Morgen von den Einzelheiten des Die
ichts verstehen konnte.Aber bald sah Karl, wen Robinson ei
ediente. In einem durch zwei Kästen vom übrigen Zimmer
ogetrennten Raum, den Karl bisher noch nicht gesehen hatte
ne große Waschung statt. Man sah den Kopf Bruneldas, den
als – das Haar war gerade ins Gesicht geschlagen – und den
res Nackens über den Kasten ragen und die hie und da geho
s Delamarche hielt einen weit herumspritzenden Badeschw
t dem Brunelda gewaschen und gerieben wurde. Man hörte
rzen Befehle des Delamarche die er dem Robinson erteilte, c
rch den jetzt verstellten eigentlichen Zugang des Raumes di
chte, sondern auf eine kleine Lücke zwischen einem Kasten
er spanischen Wand angewiesen war, wobei er überdies bei
ndreichung den Arm weit ausstrecken und das Gesicht abge
ten mußte. "Das Handtuch! Das Handtuch", rief Delamarche.
m erschrak Robinson, der gerade unter dem Tisch etwas an
hte, über diesen Auftrag und zog den Kopf unter dem Tisch
ß es schon: "Wo bleibt das Wasser, zum Teufel", und über dem
hien hochgereckt das wütende Gesicht des Delamarche.

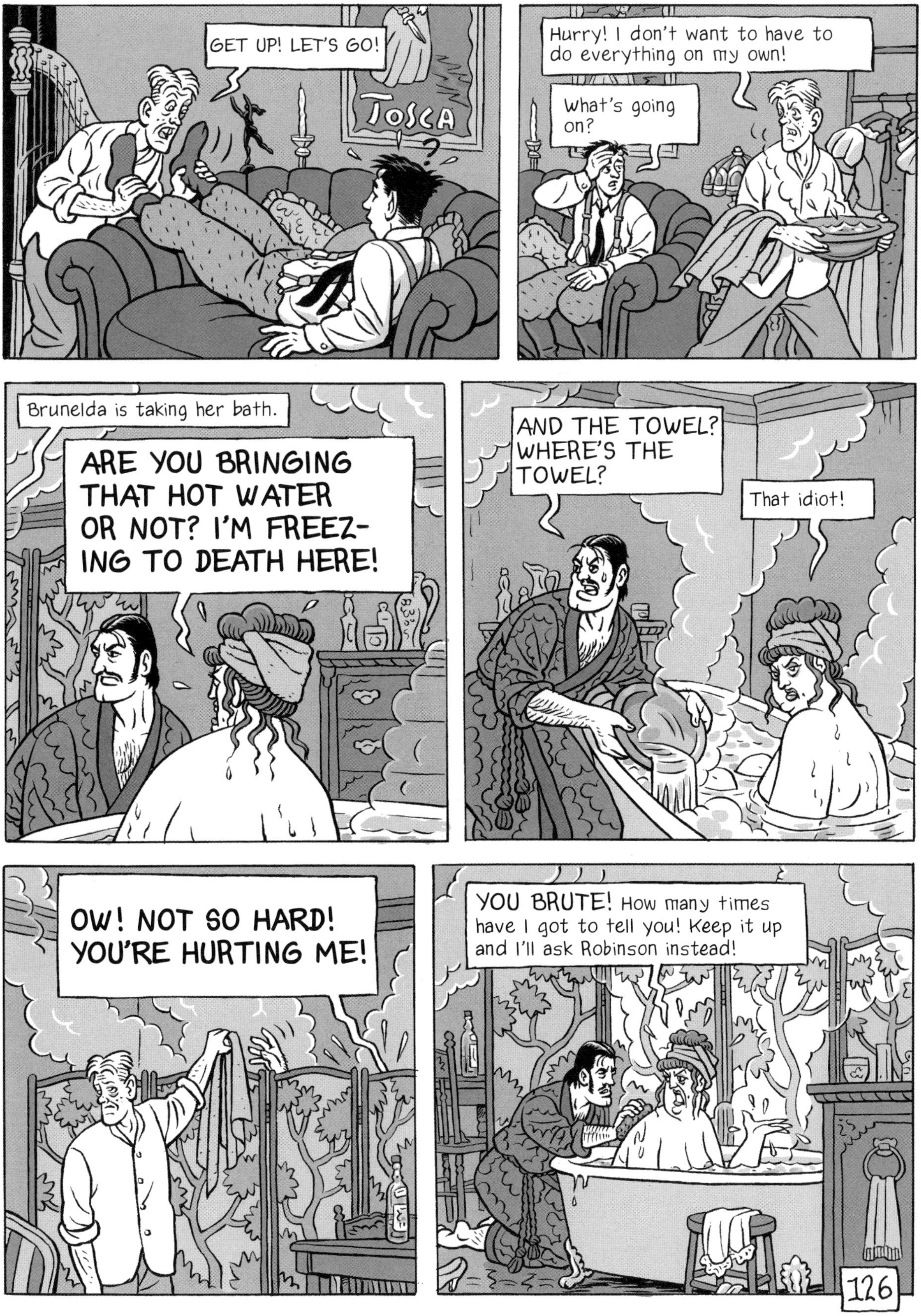
GET UP! LET'S GO!
Hurry! I don't want to have to do everything on my own!
What's going on?
Brunelda is taking her bath.
ARE YOU BRINGING THAT HOT WATER OR NOT? I'M FREEZ-ING TO DEATH HERE!
AND THE TOWEL? WHERE'S THE TOWEL?
That idiot!
OW! NOT SO HARD! YOU'RE HURTING ME!
YOU BRUTE! How many times have I got to tell you! Keep it up and I'll ask Robinson instead!
126

ROBINSOOOOON! Come scrub my back!

There's no way I'm going in...

The last time I went, they made me regret it. I'm not gonna forget that anytime soon.

PEEPING TOM! DIRTY PERVERT!

PLOOF

Gbllb

DELAMARCHE! Rub harder, for God's sake! I can't feel A THING!

There, is this better?

Hee hee! Delamarche, you're crazy! Hee hee!

It's so quiet in there...

He must be kissing her now...

All right, I'll clean up a bit then.

What's he doing? He'll wreck the place! Delamarche, tell the boy not to touch anything!

127

Hey, k... COME BACK! DON'T LEAVE ME ALONE!!

My perfume. Tell them to bring my perfume!

THE PERFUME! MAKE IT QUICK!

Any idea where she keeps her perfume?

Not a clue.

WHERE IS IT?

MY PERFUME! I WANT MY PERFUME!!

THIS INSTANT!!

ARE YOU JUST PRETENDING OR WHAT?!

If I knew what the bottle looks like...

Where is it??

128

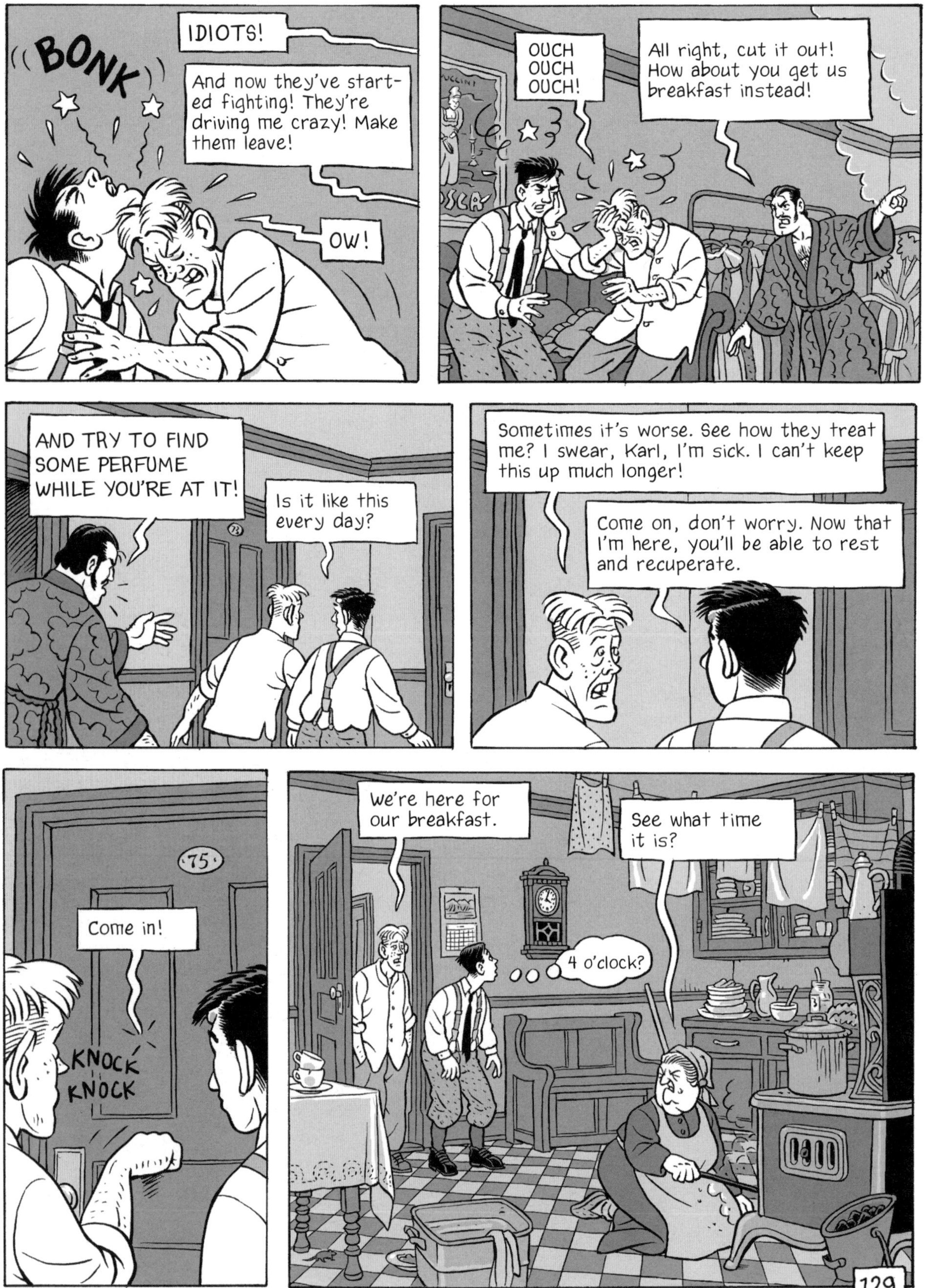
BONK
IDIOTS!
And now they've started fighting! They're driving me crazy! Make them leave!
OW!
OUCH OUCH OUCH!
All right, cut it out! How about you get us breakfast instead!
AND TRY TO FIND SOME PERFUME WHILE YOU'RE AT IT!
Is it like this every day?
Sometimes it's worse. See how they treat me? I swear, Karl, I'm sick. I can't keep this up much longer!
Come on, don't worry. Now that I'm here, you'll be able to rest and recuperate.
75
Come in!
KNOCK KNOCK
We're here for our breakfast.
See what time it is?
4 o'clock?
129

You're gonna hafta siddown and wait. I got other things to do.

Kof kof kof

We don't have much choice. We rent the room from her, so she can turn us out anytime...

What a day! My daughter's sick, I gotta do everything myself. And now this damn coal won't light! No way supper's gonna be ready on time! So if you think I've got time to deal with you...

Kof kof kof!

KETING KETING

Listen, ma'am, I know it's a bit late, but we are your tenants after all...

?

Of course, I understand that under the circumstances, you're overwhelmed today. If you don't mind, we could put together a breakfast on our own from the leftovers I see lying around.

Huh?!?

Here, hold this!

There, that'll do... Now get outta my hair, both of you!

KLANG

KLING

130

Give me the tray.

?

Hmm

Voilà!

I don't see why you went to all that trouble. It's already a hundred times better than what we usually get!

Do you think we can go in?

Looks all right. He's brushing her hair.

DELAMARCHE!! What are you trying to do? TEAR OFF MY HEAD?!?

131

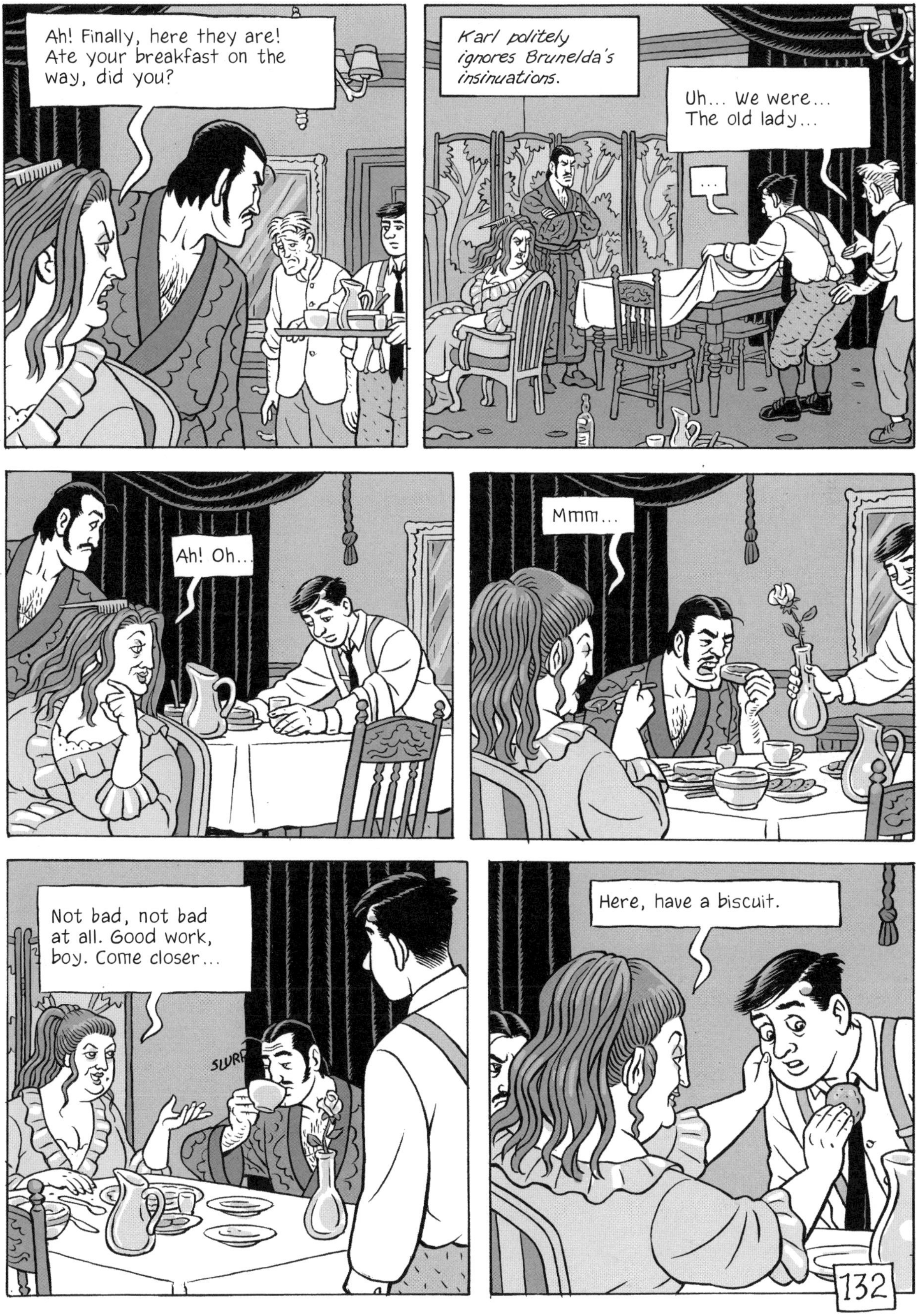
Ah! Finally, here they are! Ate your breakfast on the way, did you?
Karl politely ignores Brunelda's insinuations.
Uh... We were... The old lady...
...
Ah! Oh...
Mmm...
Not bad, not bad at all. Good work, boy. Come closer...
SLURP
Here, have a biscuit.
132

In just a few weeks, Karl manages to do the seemingly impossible: he puts some order into the apartment and wins Brunelda's respect.

Robinson uses his free time to recover.

Delamarche, meanwhile, is always arguing with Brunelda, mostly about Karl.

Karl darling here, Karl honey there... Think I haven't noticed the way you stroke his chin?

Look at you — jealous of a kid! You're a real prize, know that?

A kid that's on the lam! Wait and see if the cops don't show up here one of these day!

Let 'em come! I've got a thing or two to tell them! Think I don't know about your little schemes?

I pulled you out of the gutter and I can throw you back in!

But Delamarche won't give her the satisfaction of turning him out. One morning....

AAAAAAAHH

?!

DELAMARCHE!!!

The two swindlers are gone, along with most of Brunelda's money and valuables.

133

Shattered by her lover's betrayal, Brunelda sinks into a deep depression.

Boo hoo hoo hoo

He'll never come back!

Delamarche, my love, how could you abandon me?

MAAARCELLL!

Here, Brunelda, give it a try. You need to eat something, it'll do you good.

Maybe you're right...

Sniff

And so Brunelda, having cried herself out, turns to food to dull her grief, devouring plateful...

... after plateful.

The more massive she becomes, the more her savings dwindle.

I haven't been paid in a month, but that's not the problem. How will we cover the rent?

134

145

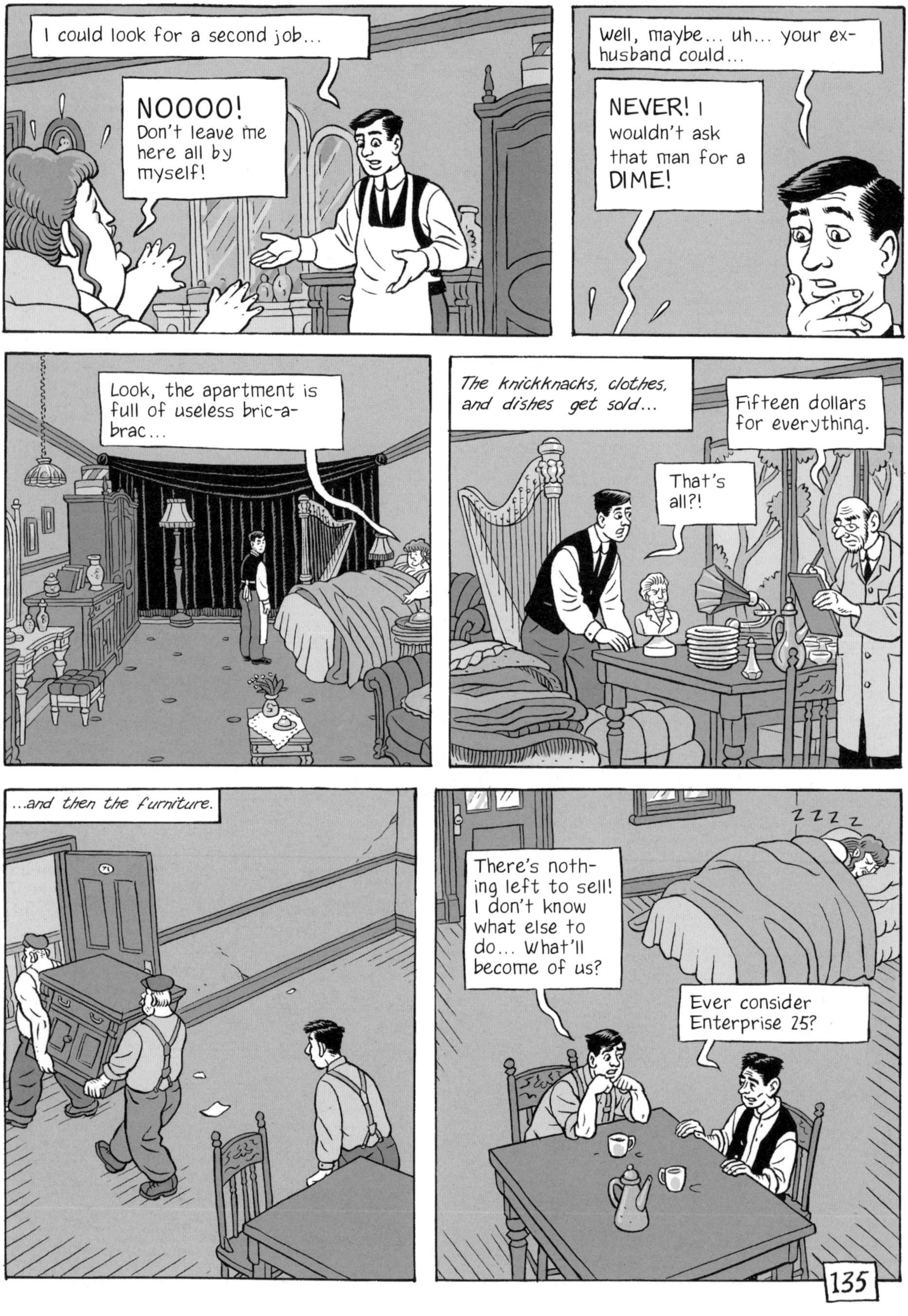
I could look for a second job...
NOOOO! Don't leave me here all by myself!
Well, maybe... uh... your ex-husband could...
NEVER! I wouldn't ask that man for a DIME!
Look, the apartment is full of useless bric-a-brac...
The knickknacks, clothes, and dishes get sold...
Fifteen dollars for everything.
That's all?!
...and then the furniture.
ZZZZ
There's nothing left to sell! I don't know what else to do... What'll become of us?
Ever consider Enterprise 25?
135

Enterprise 25? What's that?

Well, everyone's heard of it, but nobody actually knows what goes on there...

Except that it takes in obese people and offers a small sum of money in exchange. There's no news from them afterward...

But, that... that's criminal!

Who knows? The company seems to enjoy protection from high up. It might be a charitable foundation...

...but some people think it's a high-level science laboratory...

...and others say Enterprise 25 is actually a kind of luxury brothel, for clients with peculiar tastes...

— That's disgusting!
— But they're all just rumours...

I would NEVER take part in any kind of trade in human flesh!

What other choice do you have?

?!

He's right, Karl.

It's the only way out. I don't want to become a burden to you! You're young — you have your whole life ahead of you. Mine is almost over. There's no reason to hesitate.

I'll make the necessary arrangements.

And so, one winter morning...

Seven stories to go down...

This is going to be quite a feat.

Easy does it...

137

Two hours later, sweating despite the morning cold, Karl and the student finally step out onto the sidewalk with their charge.

And I was hoping to leave early so we wouldn't get noticed!

Well, I think it's time to say goodbye.

So long, Brunelda. I know we haven't always been on the best of terms, but...

I sincerely hope that you find peace where you're going.

It's all in the past now.

Good bye, Karl, and good luck. I'm sure you'll make your way all right.

Good bye. And thank you.

138

And now I need to get there as quickly and discreetly as possible.... I just hope the wheelchair holds up!

Mind telling me what you've got there?

Uh... Apples, sir.

Is that so? Apples? Think I'm a fool? Tell me who you are and where you're going!

Everything's in order, officer, I swear. We received a notice and...

Mind showing me the notice?

Of course, officer, right away...

I... I can't remember where I put the paper!

All right, that's enough!

I promise, sir, we've got the paper and we'll find it for you!

139

150

Ah! Here it is!

Oh-ho! I see... THAT's where you're taking this little miss...

Fine, you can go.

Phew!

At last...

Here it is!

Ah, it's you! You're late...

Yes, I know. We had some trouble on the way...

Don't they all.

Well hello, little miss! And welcome!

140

Young man, this is where you turn back. Here is the money, as per our agreement.

I don't want a penny of it, sir! Give it all to Brunelda!

No, Karl, the money is rightfully yours. It doesn't even cover what I owe you. Take it, you'll need it.

In any event, this little lady won't be needing money here.

...if you insist...

Now go, Karl, quickly. I can't stand goodbyes.

And Karl finds himself alone once more, with no family, legal status, papers or resources, and no cash in his pockets except the few dollars he was given for Brunelda.

He picks up odd jobs here and there to get by, but the work is miserable and the pay is poor...

Hey negro! Move yer ass!

Negro? Is that me?

Ha ha!

141

...and every day he wonders how he's managed to sink so low...

142

153

Chapter 9:
The Grand Nature Theater of Oklahoma

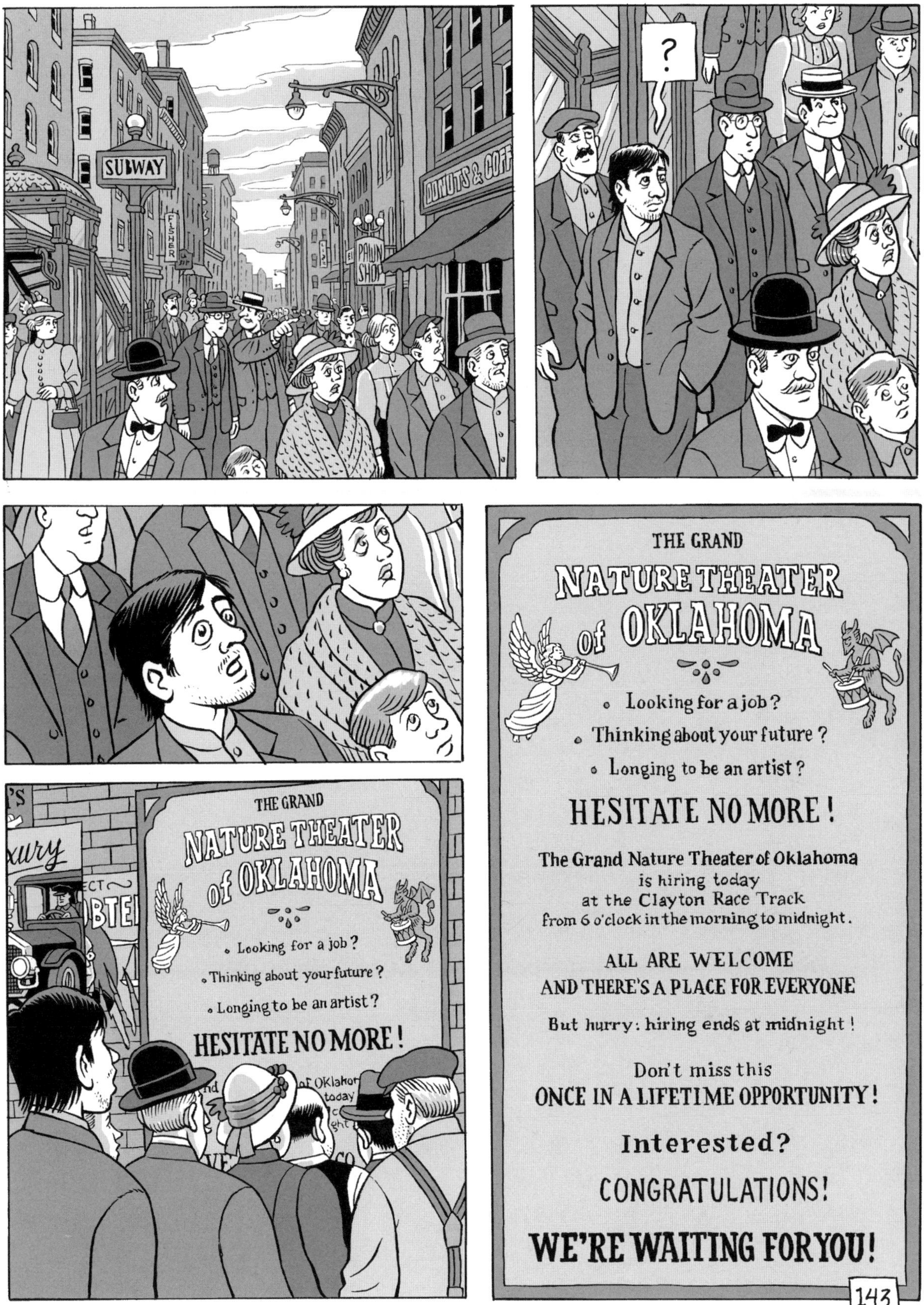
SUBWAY
DONUTS & COFF
PAWN SHOP
FISHER
?
THE GRAND
NATURE THEATER
of OKLAHOMA
• Looking for a job?
• Thinking about your future?
• Longing to be an artist?
HESITATE NO MORE!
THE GRAND
NATURE THEATER
of OKLAHOMA
• Looking for a job?
• Thinking about your future?
• Longing to be an artist?
HESITATE NO MORE!
The Grand Nature Theater of Oklahoma
is hiring today
at the Clayton Race Track
from 6 o'clock in the morning to midnight.
ALL ARE WELCOME
AND THERE'S A PLACE FOR EVERYONE
But hurry: hiring ends at midnight!
Don't miss this
ONCE IN A LIFETIME OPPORTUNITY!
Interested?
CONGRATULATIONS!
WE'RE WAITING FOR YOU!
143

...all are welcome...

It doesn't even say how much they're paying!

Yeah...the life of an artist is never enough to live on!

...a place for everyone...

All I've got left is change for one subway fare...

I suppose I could walk to Clayton...

But that would take at least three hours. If I show up late, there might not be any jobs left...

144

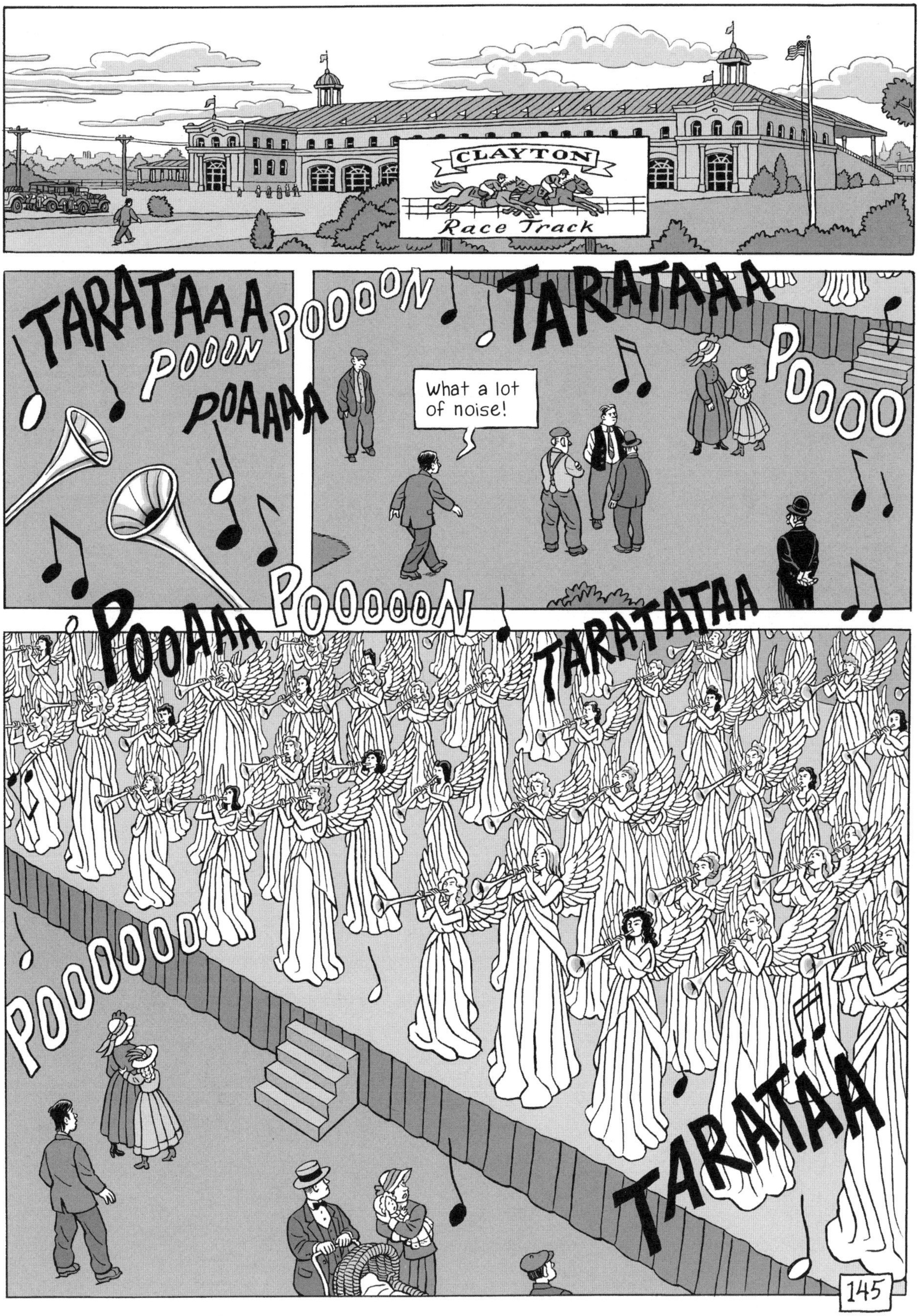
CLAYTON
Race Track
TARATAAA
POOON
POAAAA
POOOON
TARATAAA
POOOO
What a lot of noise!
POAAAA
POOOOON
TARATATAA
POOOOOOO
TARATAA
145

IS THIS WHERE THEY'RE HIRING FOR THE THEATER?

SEEMS THAT WAY. BUT WE'VE STOOD HERE FOR AN HOUR AND THERE'S BEEN NO ANNOUNCEMENTS...

Maybe they're waiting for more people to show up.

Could be...

Would you mind going inside for us to find out?

But... I'd have to cross the stage and...

Uh...

Fine then... I'll go.

KARL!

!?

146

It really is you! I'm so happy to see you!

...Fanny?

Come on up!

Can I?

Of course. Why not?

Just try not to fall, all right?

You're playing trumpet for the Grand Nature Theater of Oklahoma now?

Yes! It's a lot of fun. Want to try?

POUEEE

What an artist!

You've got real talent! You should get yourself hired as a trumpet player.

They take men too?

Yes, the men play right after us, dressed as devils. There are also a few drummers.

And they do all this just to recruit workers?

Yup!

147

159

That's incredible! Is it a new theater?

Not at all! The Grand Theater of Oklahoma has been around for ages, but it keeps getting bigger. It's the biggest theater in the world! Recruiting teams like ours travel across the whole country looking for candidates.

But why at a race track?

Because they need a lot of room for their hiring offices. They set them up in the betting booths. I hear there are almost two hundred of them.

I wonder why they've gone to so much trouble. There's not many people.

No, there's hardly anybody...

Maybe this production with all you angels and devils frightens more people than it attracts.

Maybe... You should mention it to management.

I better wait till I get hired before I start criticising.

That's true...but I'm sure they'll take you.

You really should go introduce yourself. And I need to start playing again. My break is over. Let me know how it goes!

Of course, I promise!

148

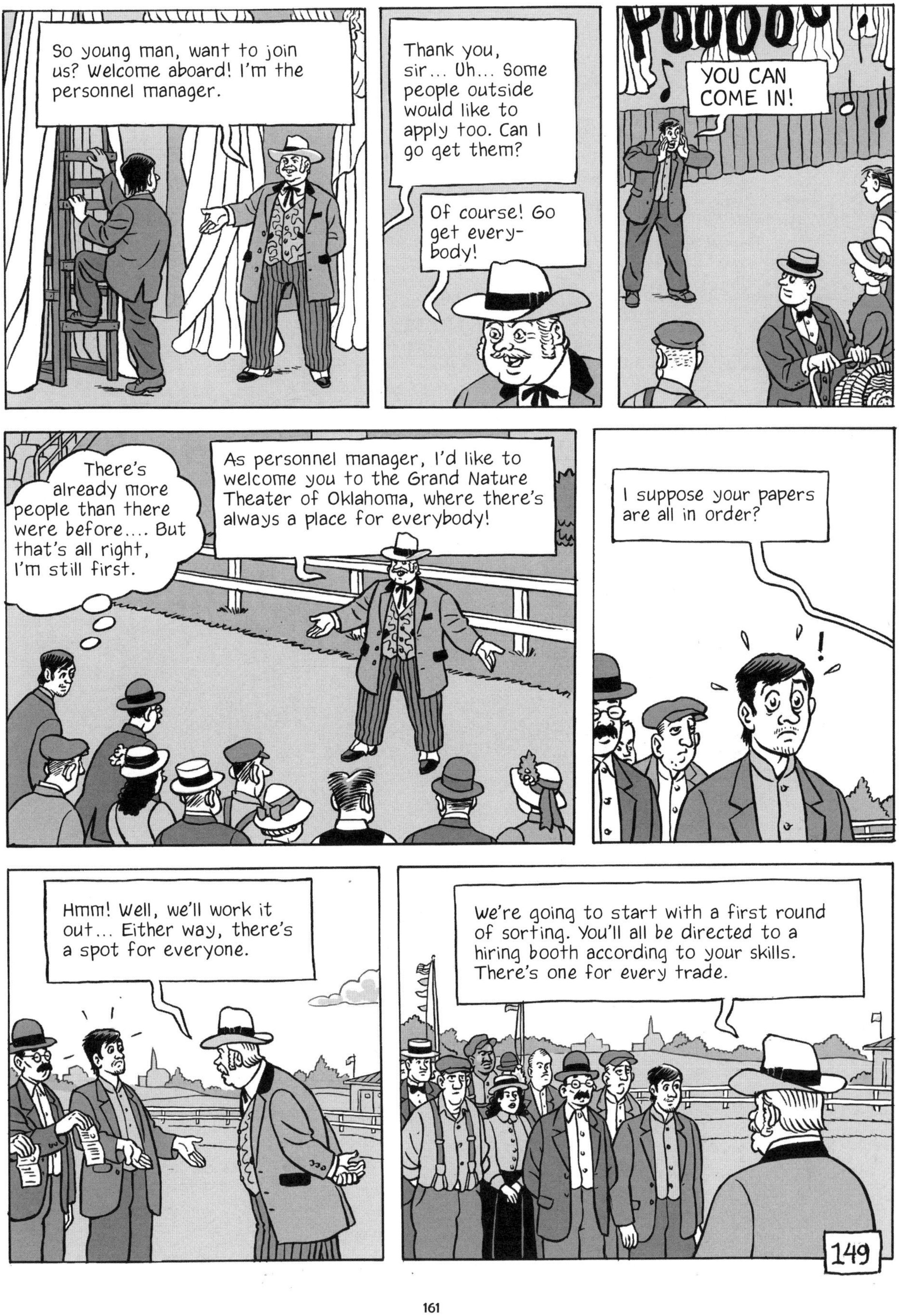

So young man, want to join us? Welcome aboard! I'm the personnel manager.
Thank you, sir... Uh... Some people outside would like to apply too. Can I go get them?
Of course! Go get every-body!
YOU CAN COME IN!
There's already more people than there were before.... But that's all right, I'm still first.
As personnel manager, I'd like to welcome you to the Grand Nature Theater of Oklahoma, where there's always a place for everybody!
I suppose your papers are all in order?
Hmm! Well, we'll work it out... Either way, there's a spot for everyone.
We're going to start with a first round of sorting. You'll all be directed to a hiring booth according to your skills. There's one for every trade.
149

All right, let's get started. Any engineers out there?

Really? You're all engineers?

That's what I figured...

At this point, it hardly matters... Anyway, I always wanted to be an engineer.

Euh... Ben... Hem!

Very good. The clerk will direct you to the hiring booth for engineers.

Your identification papers, please.

Uh... I don't have them on me, unfortunately.

ENGINEERS

...unfortunately does not have his papers.

150

So, you're an engineer?

Actually, not yet... I was studying to become one.

Then you need to go to the booth for people with scientific expertise.

28

ENGINEERS

Next.

Right this way.

What kind of scientific expertise do you have?

Well, I was studying to become an engineer...

You're in the wrong place. Go see the booth for secondary school graduates.

Where and when did you graduate?

Actually, I had to, uh... interrupt my studies...

Go to the booth for secondary school students, then...

...and where did you study?

It was in Europe, at...

Europe? That's a whole other story!

In that case, you need to go to the booth for former students of European secondary schools. It's over there, at the very end of the row.

151

You have no papers?

No.

Name, please.

K... Uh... Negro.

...has no papers...

199

...Negro...

What's this? His name can't possibly be Negro!!

Makes no difference.

Take this and introduce yourself to the director. He is in the judges' booth, at the top of the stands.

...I'm telling you, I'm sure his name isn't Negro...

MR KALLA
SALESMAN
MRS KALLA
& CHILD

Were you hired?

Yes, just now. What an amazing company! It's all so well organized!

Wonderful! Congratulations!

Good luck to you, too.

152

Come in, young man.

Your name is Negro, you're a former student of a European secondary school, and you're applying for a job as an actor. Is that correct?

Actor?

Uh... yes, right.

You're unemployed?

Yes, sir, I am.

Where did you last work?

For the railway.

Did you like your job?

No.

I see... What kind of work do you consider yourself suited for?

Well... I saw on the poster that you have jobs for everybody.

We know that.

Of course... Uh... Well, actually, sir, I'm not sure I'm cut out to be an actor. But I'd be happy to do anything I'm asked to do.

What were you studying? In Europe, I mean.

I wanted to be an engineer.

Needless to say, you can't work as an engineer immediately. You seem sturdy, though. Maybe a lower level job as a mechanic or a machinist would do for now.

Yes, sir, absolutely! That would be perfect!

It's settled, then. You'll be a machinist.

Welcome to the theater, young man.

153

I can't wait to tell Fanny the good news!

The musicians? They left just over an hour ago...

Too bad. One of the angels is a friend of mine...

You'll see her again in Oklahoma.

Better hurry, or you'll miss the banquet!

The banquet?

Looks like I'm the last one here.

...and now, a toast to our beloved Director, whose staunch...

154

...BEACON of the working class, FATHER of the unemployed...

GIACOMO !?!

KARL ROSSMANN! Come sit over here, there's a free spot!

...who has welcomed HIC! us with open arms into the great family of this illustrious theater, where... uh...

I don't believe it! Who would have thought I'd find you here...

You haven't changed a bit since the Occidental Hotel!

Copious amounts of food are served and the wine flows freely. Photos of the Grand Nature Theater of Oklahoma are handed out to the diners.

Look! The Presidential Box!

155

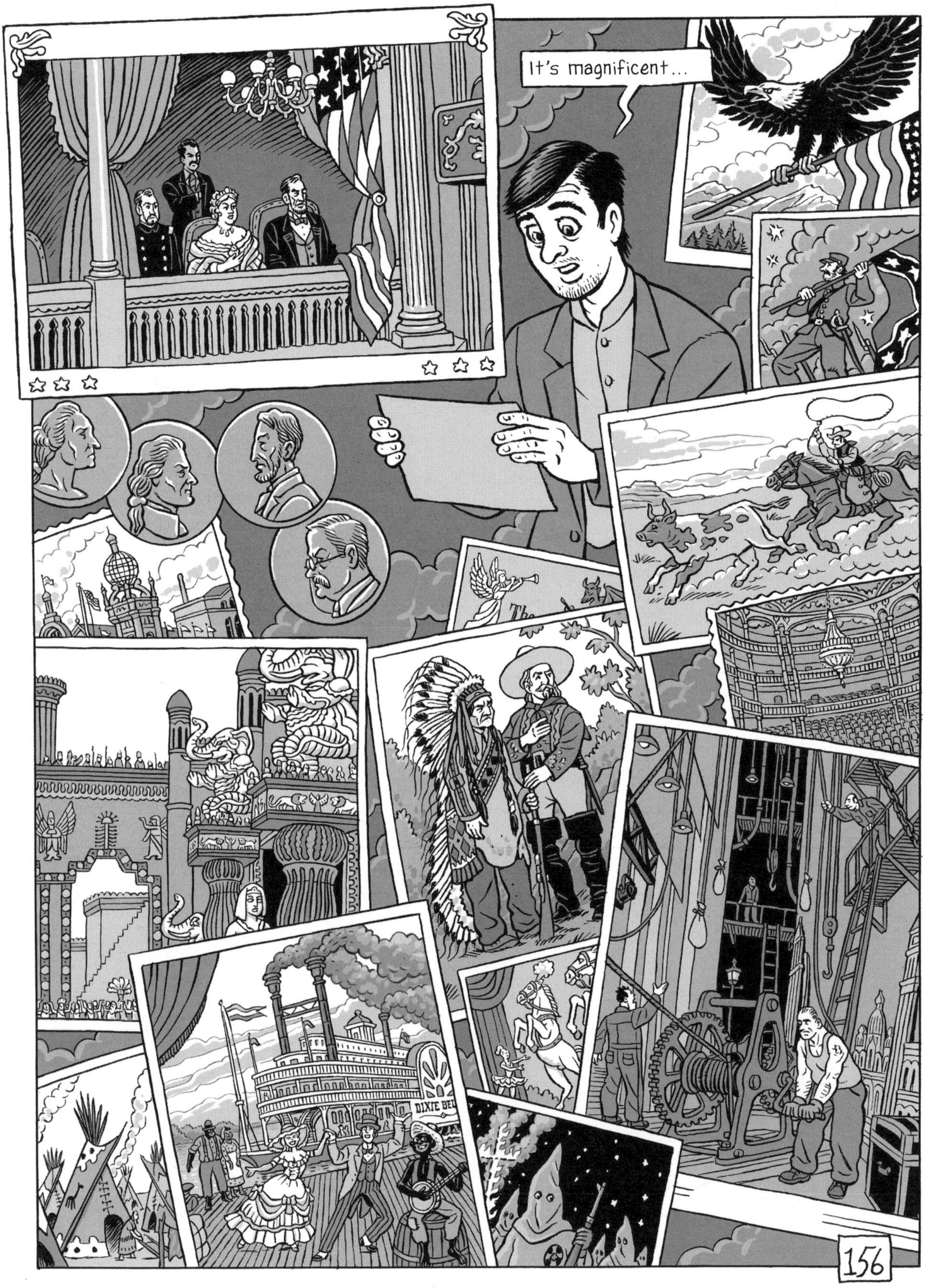
It's magnificent...
156

...and please accept our g... HIC! gratitude for this generous and ssumptuous feast......

Sorry to interrupt the festivities, folks, but it's time to go!

YES, you really know how to win a man's HEART!

All right, BREAK IT UP! The train is leaving in ten minutes!

Bravo!

CLAP
CLAP
CLAP CLAP

Ha ha!

...and I raise my glass once more to...

COME ON, FOLKS! LET'S GO! THE TRAIN'S NOT GONNA WAIT!

ALL ABOARD!

YTON

TOOOOO

23741

5072

157

169

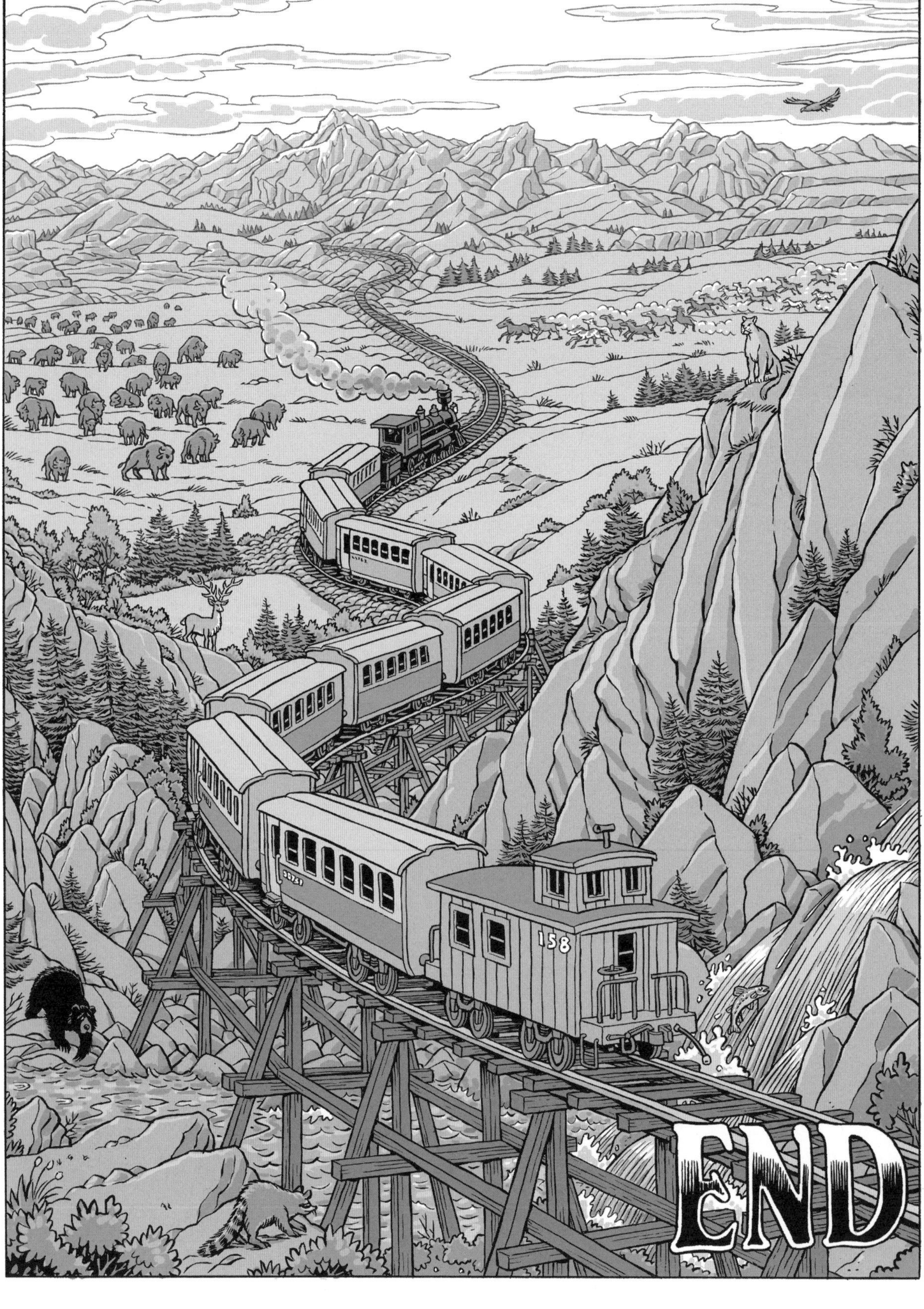
158
END

Supplement:
THE NEW LAWYER

THE NEW LAWYER

CLOP CLOP CLOP CLOP CLOP

Who's that?

It's Doctor Bucephalus, our new lawyer.

CLOP CLOP CLOP

!?

CLAC

Bucephalus? You mean the famous Bucephalus?

None other.

CLOP CLOP CLOP

Réal Godbout

1

I wouldn't have recognized him. I didn't even know he's a lawyer now...

CLOP CLOP

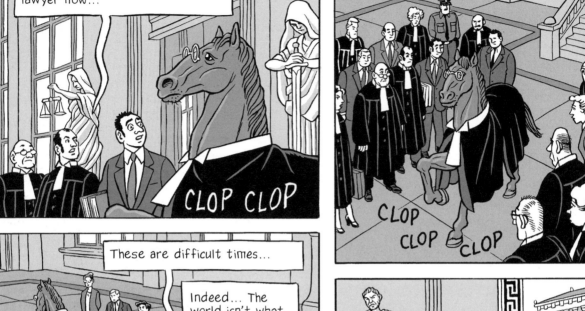

CLOP CLOP CLOP

These are difficult times...

Indeed... The world isn't what it used to be.

CLOP CLOP CLOP

The days are long gone...

ΔΗΜΟΣΘΕΝΗΣ

...when Bucephalus served Alexander of Macedonia in battle...

2

And the likes of Alexander the Great are gone too...

We still know how to kill, though. We're still able to drive a spear through a friend across the banquet table.

Many people believe Macedonia is too small, and they curse King Philip, the father.

But nobody, NOBODY, is able to lead the way to India!

The gates of India were already out of reach in Alexander's time, but at least the mighty conqueror pointed the way with his sword.

3

Today, those gates have been moved to higher and more distant places. And there is no one left to show us the way...

Many people brandish swords, but they only wave them about, confusing the gaze of those who might want to follow them.

CLOP CLOP CLOP CLOP

CLOP CLOP CLOP CLOP

Based on a story by Franz Kafka

4

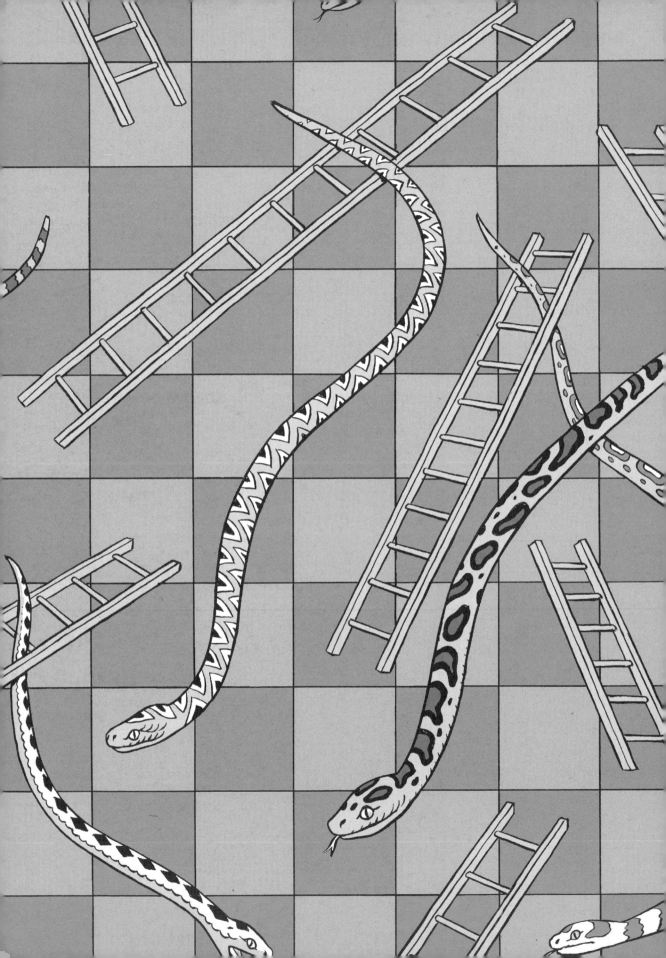